Design

George H. Marcus

in the Fifties

Design in the Fifties

George H. Marcus

When Everyone Went Modern

Prestel

Munich · New York

For Nancy

© 1998 by Prestel-Verlag, Munich and New York,
and George H. Marcus

gns,
on,

Picasso

1954
(see fig. 44). "Golden Triangle" carafe, advertisement for Inland
Glass (see fig. 104).
Half-title page: Plastic laminate, detail of a flowerpot stand,
German, 1950s. Stadtmuseum Trostberg.
Frontispiece: Chair designed by Charles Eames (American),
1948. Fiberglass, steel, and wood. Made by Herman Miller.
Philadelphia Museum of Art. Gift of COLLAB: The Contemporary
Design Group for the Philadelphia Museum of Art.

Library of Congress Cataloging-in-Publication Data
Marcus, George H.
Design in the fifties : when everyone went modern /
George H. Marcus.
p. 160 cm. 16.5 x 23.5
Includes bibliographical references and index.
ISBN 3-7913-1939-6 (alk. paper)
1. Design–History–20th Century. I. Title.
NK 1390.M27 1998
745.2'09'04–dc21
98-2743 CIP

Prestel-Verlag
Mandlstraße 26, D-80802 Munich, Germany
Tel. (+49-89) 38 17 09-0; Fax (+49-89) 38 17 09-35 and
16 West 22nd Street, New York, NY 10010, USA
Tel. (212) 627-8199; Fax (212) 627-9866

Prestel books are available worldwide. Please contact your
nearest bookseller or write to either of the above addresses for
information concerning your local distributor.

Edited by Judith Gilbert
Designed by Matthias Hauer
Lithography by Repro Ludwig, Zell am See
Printed and bound by Wagner GmbH, Nördlingen

Printed in Germany using ecologically-safe ink
and acid-free paper

ISBN 3-7913-1939-6

Contents

Modern in the Fifties

To be modern, design did not just have to be new, it had to be free of any reference to the decorative styles of the past, which at the beginning of the postwar period were still preferred by most people for the furnishing of their homes (fig. 2). About this, every definition and interpretation of modern was adamant. "We do *not* approve," admonished a 1948 editorial in *Interiors,* an American magazine committed to modern design, "of the voice and the face of Bing Crosby suddenly emerging from something that looks like a Sheraton breakfront. We do *not* approve," the editorial continued, "of a Georgian dining room, no matter how beautifully reproduced, on the 32nd floor of a skyscraper hotel."[1] Ever since the middle of the previous century, reformers had condemned design's dependence on historicism (and its handmaiden, ornamentalism), and the progress of modern design could be measured by the extent to which the mining of historic styles was supplanted by the creation of new, anonymous, and universal forms, forms that looked to the future instead of the past. And because after the Second World War everyone wanted to put the past behind them, modern design caught on quickly, succeeding across broader class barriers and greater distances than might ever have been reasonably expected.

The turn toward modern began immediately after the war in the United States, which had suffered least from its deprivations and had begun to rebound almost as soon as the fighting was over. But the need to be modern was felt everywhere, from Great Britain to Japan, as the industrialized nations worked their way through wartime recovery; and although they shared an international vocabulary of forms and their eyes were never turned for long from America, they arrived at

1   "Masks," printed fabric designed by Ray Komai (American), c. 1948. Made by Laverne International. Montreal Museum of Decorative Arts. Gift of Helen Fioratti.

their own, individual understanding of what modernity meant. Postwar modern design was not dependent on any single look or approach, nor on any one philosophy. It embraced such divergent elements as a revived admiration for the values of handcraftsmanship, the geometric machine style that had emerged in the 1920s, organic shapes from the 1930s, and sculptural forms and abstract patterning derived from the fine arts — joined with a bright, optimistic palette, and as the decade wore on, a hard automotive glitter — to create a modern design

2   Advertisement for Admiral television, 1951.

that was broad, up-to-date, and inclusive, and for the most part free of the stylistic and decorative influences of the past.

But for some partisans of modern design — professionals mainly, architects, designers, critics, publishers, pedagogues, and museum curators — repudiating historic styles and elaborate ornamentation was only one part of being modern. Contemporary traditionalists tied to the ideas of prewar European modernism, they rejected the street definition of modern as anything that was new and up-to-date for a definition that restricted the term to those works that also satisfied a specific set of aesthetic and moral dictates, and for them modern could be many decades old. These principles reverberate back to the mid-nineteenth century in England, when reformers began to advocate a design that was simple, economical, and utilitarian as an antidote to the great mass of manufactured goods catering to the taste of the public for elaborate decoration in historical styles that the industrial revolution had made possible. They were codified for postwar readers by Edgar Kaufmann, Jr., as the "Twelve Precepts of Modern Design," published in *What is Modern Design?* in 1950 by the Museum of Modern Art in New York:

1. Modern design should fulfill the practical needs of modern life.
2. Modern design should express the spirit of our times.
3. Modern design should benefit by contemporary advances in the fine arts and pure sciences.
4. Modern design should take advantage of new materials and techniques and develop familiar ones.

5. Modern design should develop the forms, textures and colors that spring from the direct fulfillment of requirements in appropriate materials and techniques.
6. Modern design should express the purpose of an object, never making it seem to be what it is not.
7. Modern design should express the qualities and beauties of the materials used, never making the materials seem to be what they are not.
8. Modern design should express the methods used to make an object, not disguising mass production as handicraft or simulating a technique not used.
9. Modern design should blend the expression of utility, materials and process into a visually satisfactory whole.
10. Modern design should be simple, its structure, evident in its appearance, avoiding extraneous enrichment.
11. Modern design should master the machine for the service of man.
12. Modern design should serve as wide a public as possible, considering modest needs and limited costs no less challenging than the requirements of pomp and luxury.[2]

In his booklet Kaufmann, then a research associate at the museum, illustrated works that dated from as early as the end of the nineteenth century alongside those that came from more recent times. His selection included both handmade objects, such as turn-of-the-century iridescent glass by the American designer Louis Comfort Tiffany and Oriental-inspired stoneware from the 1930s by the British potter Bernard Leach, and industrially manufactured products, such as a modular plastic, plywood, and metal storage system from the 1940s designed by the American Charles Eames (color plate 4). Clearly excluded were objects embellished with applied ornament or imitative decoration ("extraneous enrichment" was his euphemism), although decoration was allowed

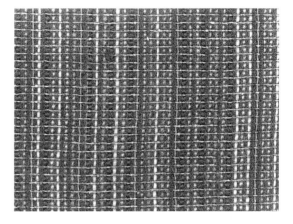

3 Upholstery fabric designed by Evelyn Hill (American), 1951. Wool, viscose, rayon, and synthetic raffia. Philadelphia Museum of Art. Gift of Mr. and Mrs. George Anselvicius.

when it arose from the structure of an object, for example, patterns created by combining different materials, colors, and techniques in weaving (fig. 3), or when it fulfilled an object's function. Thus, such designs as those printed on fabrics and wallpapers were permitted (as long as they were abstract or suitably stylized; fig. 1) following the justification voiced by the American textile designer Angelo Testa that when the function of an object was "purely decorative" its ornamental patterning was its purpose,[3] and thus could not be considered "extraneous."

One of Kaufmann's picture spreads featured eight chairs that brought together two distinct episodes of modern design (fig. 4). The four in the top row were elegant, geometric works from the 1920s and 1930s created in Germany by Marcel Breuer and Ludwig Mies van der Rohe and in Holland by J. J. P. Oud. With their simple, unadorned, machine-inspired aesthetic, these shiny, steel chairs were emblematic of a reductive philosophy of timeless design known as "functionalism."[4] They represented the height of European modernism, and the designs by Breuer and Mies had already been almost universally acknowledged as icons of early twentieth-century design. The four in the bottom row, from the late 1930s and the 1940s, were more complex, curvilinear designs by the Americans Eero Saarinen and Charles Eames and the Argentinian design group Bonnet, Kurchan, and Ferrari-Hardoy. Created by the next generation of modern designers, these molded-plastic, molded-plywood, and welded-metal chairs were already well on their way to attaining the status of icons from a subsequent period.

The works illustrated in Kaufmann's booklet, which brought prewar modernist design up to date by broadening its aesthetic vision to

4   Chairs, from *What Is Modern Design?* by Edgar Kaufmann, Jr., published by the Museum of Modern Art, New York, in 1950.

include objects created with newly popular organic forms and the benefit of new technology, formed an irreproachable nucleus of spare and utilitarian products that became the typological ideal of modern design for decades to come. Kaufmann's model was able to co-opt the definition of modern because virtually the only continuing examination of contemporary industrial production emanated from the exhibitions and publications of such American institutions as the Museum of Modern Art and the Walker Art Center in Minneapolis, which subscribed to the modernist aesthetic.

Their preference for design that was simple, austere, and objective set the pattern for much of what was presented during the 1950s as modern furnishings in magazines, advertisements (color plate 1), and retail shops, although these designs followed a somewhat less authoritarian — and more practical — concept, which was known as "good design." The underlying aesthetic approach espoused by forward-looking designers and manufacturers in every industrialized country, good design attempted to establish standards for everyday products that were to appeal to the population at large and, in accordance with the paternalistic goals from the previous century, improve their lives. With standards that were less stringent than those enumerated by Kaufmann and less concerned with abstract principles, good design was geared to the marketplace. Products were not necessarily the "*best* in design," as *Interiors* pointed out in 1948, but those that could be commercially competitive; accordingly, "consensus of opinion — based on appearance, facility and economy of manufacture, and sales appeal"[5] somehow established what good design encompassed.

The principles of good design had considerable impact on everything from automobiles to interiors as manufacture resumed in the immediate postwar period. But later, with the advent of an economy geared more and more to mass consumption, some products exploiting the modern vocabulary began to exceed the boundaries of good design with the introduction of energetic surface decoration, brash colors, and metallic glitter in order to compete for the attention of a wider and less sophisticated audience. It was not so much the forms of these products as the way their forms were created (with applied veneers, plastic laminates, and imitation materials) and decorated (with a cacophony of colors and an audacity of ornament) that clashed most heavily with good design. By the middle of the decade, almost anything — even tradition — had become fair game for modern design, resulting in the multiplicity of modes that characterized the 1950s — and its subsequent reputation as a time of little content and a lot of bad taste. But now, half a century later, this view has been widely reassessed. We have come to understand the value of a broader dialectic of design, one that can prize the restraint of a utility-based, socially responsible modern aesthetic as well as the exuberance of a lively, expressive, and ecumenical modern ornamental vocabulary with popular appeal — aspects of the Fifties that resonate strongly in our own postmodern era.

1   F. de N. S., "Merry Christmas!!," *Interiors*, vol. 107 (February 1948), p. 75.
2   Edgar Kaufmann, Jr., *What Is Modern Design?* (New York: The Museum of Modern Art, 1950), p. 7. Kaufmann discussed his initial reluctance to create these precepts in "The Design Shift 1950–1960," *Industrial Design*, vol. 7 (August 1960), p. 50.
3   Angelo Testa, "Design vs. Monkey Business," *Interiors*, vol. 107 (February 1948), p. 84.
4   See George H. Marcus, *Functionalist Design: An Ongoing History* (Munich/New York: Prestel, 1995).
5   "Good Design for 1949," *Interiors*, vol. 108 (December 1948), p. 114.

Color Plates

Where do you put radiators in a room this modern?

1   Advertisement for Crane radiators (detail), *House and Garden,* September 1952. Included in this good design interior are George Nelson's component "Basic Cabinet Series" (1946), Van Keppel-Green's steel and cord lounge chair and ottoman (1947), and Isamu Noguchi's free-form coffee table (*c.* 1947).

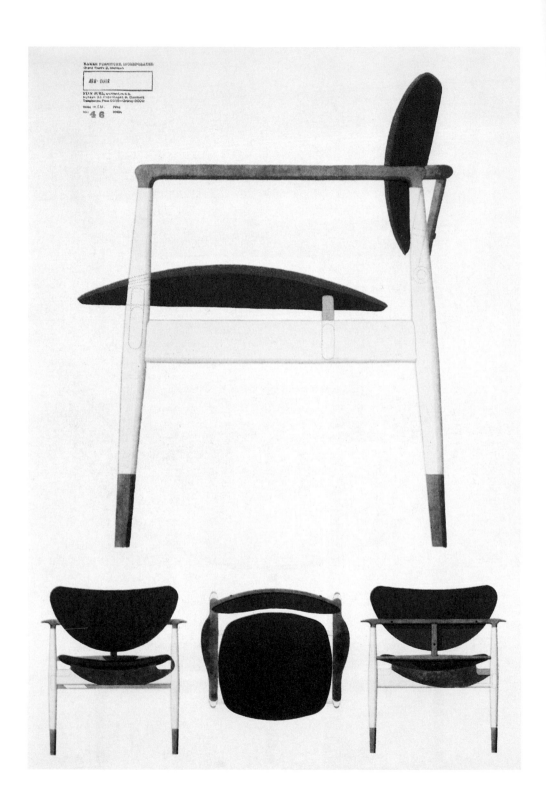

2   Drawings of an armchair designed by Finn Juhl (Danish) for Baker furniture, *Interiors,* November 1951.

3   Sketch for a living room by Jean Royère (French), 1950–51. Watercolor. Musée des Arts Décoratifs, Paris.

4   Storage unit designed by Charles Eames (American), *c.* 1949. Plastic, plywood, and metal. Made by Herman Miller. Montreal Museum of Decorative Arts. Gift of Mr. and Mrs. Robert L. Tannenbaum.

5 "Pythagoras," printed fabric designed by Sven Markelius (Swedish), 1952. Montreal Museum of Decorative Arts. Gift of Louise Armstrong in memory of Harris Armstrong.

6 "Krenit" bowl designed by Herbert Krenchel (Danish), 1953. Enameled steel. Made by Torben Ørskov. Philadelphia Museum of Art. Gift of COLLAB: The Contemporary Design Group for the Philadelphia Museum of Art.

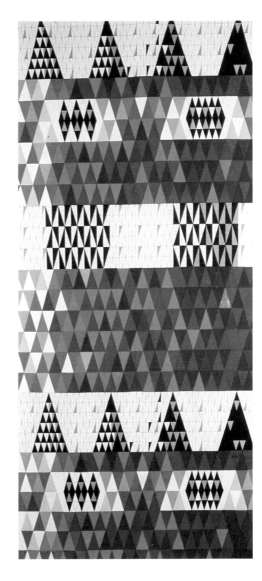

7   Vases and bowls designed by Fulvio Bianconi (Italian), Thomas Stearns (American), and Ercole Barovier (Italian), 1950–65. Blown glass. Made by Venini & Co. and Barovier e Toso. Courtesy of Barry Friedman Ltd., New York.

8   Prototype of a window blind (detail) designed by Dorothy Liebes (American), c. 1950. Bamboo, chenille, and metallic yarns. Philadelphia Museum of Art. Gift of Bonnie Cashin.

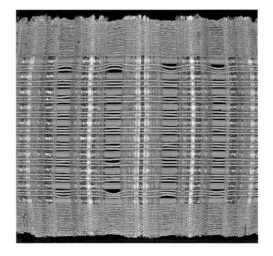

9   Chair designed by Hans J. Wegner (Danish), 1949. Oak and cane. Made by Johannes Hansen.
Courtesy Johannes Hansens Møbelsnedkeri.

10   Table, shelf, and mirror designed by Ruth Richter Hesse (German), *c.* 1952. Painted wood, mosaic, and brass. Made by Dübbers–Mosaik. Museum für Kunsthandwerk, Frankfurt.

11   Printed fabric, English, 1950s. Author's collection.

12   "Town and Country" dinnerware designed by Eva Zeisel (American), *c.* 1946. Glazed ceramic.
Made by Red Wing Pottery. Collection of Steven Beyer, Penn Valley, Pennsylvania.

13   Printed fabric, American, 1950s. Philadelphia Museum of Art. Purchased with funds contributed by an anonymous donor.

14   "Espace," printed fabric designed by Elsbeth Kupferoth (German), c. 1954. Made by Pausa. Victoria and Albert Museum, London.

15   Chair designed by Folke Jansson (Swedish), 1955–60. Vitra Design Museum Collection,
Weil am Rhein, Germany.

16 Vases, pitchers, and lamp base, *c.* 1950. Glazed ceramic. Made by Lusso. Galerie J. and F. Dewindt, Brussels.

Floor is Armstrong vinyl-asbestos Excelon Tile, Style Nos. 777 and 770.

"sundae" basement solves everyday problems

This room belongs to some of the luckiest teen-agers — and the cleverest parents — in all the world! Just last month, upstairs, it was anybody's guess who owned the living room — the high-school set or the grownups. Now everybody's happy, especially Mother. For not even dancing feet and spilled drinks will mar the gay floor of Armstrong Excelon Tile. Even popcorn sweeps up quickly, because the plastic surface is so smooth. In fact, the only real trouble you're likely to have with Excelon Tile is *choosing* it, for there are so many lovely colorings and handsome designs. Putting it down is simple . . . even paying for it is easy, for this is a really inexpensive floor. In every way, Armstrong Excelon Tile is the best of today's low-cost resilient tile floors, for every room in your home.

SEND FOR FREE BOOK, just published, "New Beauty for Basements and Basementless Houses." 16 color pages, dozens of exciting decorating ideas. Also included, description of the basement playroom shown above. Write Armstrong Cork Company, 5608 Plum Street, Lancaster, Pennsylvania.

ⒶArmstrong

THE MODERN FASHION IN

FLOORS

LINOLEUM • PLASTIC CORLON® • EXCELON® VINYL-ASBESTOS TILE • CUSTOM CORLON PLASTIC TILE • RUBBER TILE • CORK TILE • ASPHALT TILE • LINOTILE®

17   Advertisement for Armstrong floors, *American Home*, August 1956.

8 glamorous exterior colors to choose from! Select the decorator color that harmonizes with your kitchen decor—that blends with the wallpaper, paint, curtains and floor coverings. Color models have beautiful white and gold interiors. World-famous color consultants have selected FOODARAMA colors. New Kelvinator electric ranges, with disposable aluminum oven linings* and Bonus Broiler, are available in colors to match.

*PATENT APPLIED FOR.

| BERMUDA PINK | SPRING GREEN | FERN GREEN | DAWN GRAY | SAND BEIGE | BUTTERCUP YELLOW | HARVEST YELLOW | LAGOON BLUE |

AND CLASSIC WHITE—OF COURSE

18   Advertisement for Kelvinator appliances (detail), *House Beautiful,* May 1955.

19   "Royal 500" pocket transistor radio, advertisement for Zenith, *Holiday,* July 1957.

20   "Personal" television, 1956. Metal. Made by RCA Victor. Collection of Ron Kanter, Philadelphia.

Becoming Modern

In 1945, as the war was heading toward its close, an advertisement in *Life* magazine showed a young bride composing a letter to her husband in the service overseas: "When you come home to stay," she writes, subtly in rhyme, "We'll live in a kingdom all our own ... A kingdom just big enough for three ... with a picket fence for boundary. And I can picture as plain as day, ivy climbing a garden wall and smoke curling up from a tall, white chimney ... and a fanlight glowing over our front door. The door of the house we'll build ... after the war!" And because this was an advertisement for Kelvinator appliances, she continues: "And we'll follow our noses to the kitchen door. It will be like no kitchen you've ever seen before. It will be an enchanted place. ..."[1]

The young bride's dream of settling into her own picture-perfect home after the war was not quite as romantic as it might seem. Throughout the war, American planners, developers, and manufacturers had been encouraging such dreams, optimistically promoting idyllic visions of suburban houses filled with new appliances and other consumer goods that wartime restrictions had made virtually unavailable. So much conjecture and so much hyperbole marked these predictions that in 1943, Raymond Loewy, one of America's leading industrial designers, felt compelled to warn the nation against holding to these expectations: "To the scrap heap of discredited but once popular theories," he wrote in the *New York Times Magazine*, "please add another, the immediate Post-war Dream World. To be honest ... the wonderful new products will be a long time coming if they ever do. Lately it has become apparent that the public is being misinformed systematically about the wonders that await them in their dealers' windows on

5   Detail of architectural rendering of one of the first modern-style houses in Levittown, Long Island, unveiled in 1949 (see fig. 9). Nassau County Museum Collection, Long Island Studies Institute, Hempstead, New York.

the day when 'Johnnie comes marching home.' There is talk of a $300 automobile, of plywood homes that can be delivered in packing cases, revolving refrigerators that will crack ice and tenderize meats without so much as connecting a plug."[2]

Loewy was right. Cheap products with wonderful new features were a long time coming. Regardless of the spate of articles published at war's end about futuristic cars, which generally envisioned elements of aircraft design brought down to earth, and the few experimental models, such as Henry Dreyfuss's Convair automobile-airplane, that actually did so (fig. 6), the first postwar automobiles (the 1946 models) were little more than prewar designs cosmetically updated. Because of the strong consumer demand that kept the prices of these models up and the large manufacturers struggling to fill the orders they had, there was little incentive for them to redesign their cars

6   Convair autoplane designed by Henry Dreyfuss (American) and Theodore P. Hall (American), 1947. Made by Consolidated Vultee Aircraft. Cooper-Hewitt, National Design Museum, Smithsonian Institution/Art Resource, New York. Gift of Doris and Henry Dreyfuss.

over the next few years. Among the smaller manufacturers, however, alternatives to standard automotive design were being devised, most notably the dynamic 1947 Studebaker Starlight, which was newly styled with wrap-around aircraft-type windows by Loewy and Virgil Exner (later Chrysler's chief designer), and the 1948 Tucker Torpedo, the prototype of a new make with far-advanced safety features, considerable economy, and strong, sculptural lines. While the Studebaker's modern appeal was reflected in increased sales figures, the Tucker never even made it onto the market, the victim of a now widely acknowledged conspiracy among government officials and the auto industry to keep what would have become a threateningly competitive, forward-looking, and long-lasting car off the road.[3]

Cheap, prefabricated homes built with the benefits of wartime technological advances — one early hope for a quick solution to America's severe postwar housing shortage[4] — also were a long time coming because shipping of the conventionally styled structures proved too cumbersome and too expensive (they achieved sizable sales figures only in the early 1950s). Had the one truly innovative concept proposed for efficient factory-built housing entered production — the round aluminum house suspended on wires from a central assembly mast that R. Buckminster Fuller designed in 1945 (fig. 7), which *Life* magazine called the "most startling solution yet offered for the U.S. housing shortage"[5] — it would have had an incredible impact on the American landscape, challenging large numbers of potential home owners to alter their expectations from houses built with traditional floor plans, construction methods, materials,

and styles to a futuristic, function-based design that looked like no permanent house had looked before. Engineered for manufacture with the materials and techniques of the aircraft industry and for an annual production rate of sixty thousand units, these houses were to have been made in the retooled factories of the Beech Aircraft Company in Wichita, Kansas, a project that was vital to its plans for peacetime reconversion. Virtually every feature of this naturally ventilated, two-bedroom, two-bathroom, aluminum structure was new and noteworthy. Easy and cheap to transport because it was constructed from modular, light-weight components and had its own cylindrical, reusable shipping container, which solved the problems that plagued other factory-made houses, Fuller's round house could be assembled by six workers in one day. But it never went into production despite an enthusiastic public response and broad industrial support, mostly it seems because of Fuller's fanatical need to refine his design to the

7   Prototype of the prefabricated "Wichita" house designed by R. Buckminster Fuller (American), 1947. Aluminum. Copyright 1960 Allegra Fuller Snyder, courtesy Buckminster Fuller Institute, Santa Barbara. The aluminum cylinder next to the house is the reusable container in which all of the prefabricated elements were to be shipped.

point of perfection and therefore beyond the bounds of time schedules and economic feasibility.

Building Suburbia

Instead, housing in the immediate postwar period would follow more conventional forms. As a shot in the arm for an economy converting from wartime to peacetime industry, the United States government was relying heavily on the construction of new housing, particularly single-family dwellings. All over the country, but more heavily in the areas surrounding the large cities, builders began to develop new communities populated with streets and streets of similar houses. The pace of home building quickened as developers experimented with alternative construction methods (such as assembly-line site fabrication) and alternative materials (such as metal for framing) to open up large-scale tract-house developments in the new suburbs, among them Kaiser Home's Panorama City in Los Angeles and American Community Builders' Park Forest development outside Chicago. In 1947, the New York developer Levitt & Sons had introduced a program of industrial-style construction methods that each year allowed them to build thousands of cheap houses (an unheard of number for a single firm), which were set in a pattern of wide curving streets in former potato fields on the outskirts of New York City. Bolstered by new means of financing introduced by the government, such houses were sold to first-time home owners through the GI Bill of Rights, bringing a large group of new buyers into the American housing market. Young married veterans were encouraged in their dream of home ownership through the easy credit of Federal Housing Administration (FHA) financing, and the government made potential

home buyers of all returning servicemen — all, that is, except veterans of color, who were not allowed to buy in these new developments and who had difficulty finding other housing possibilities that were considered good mortgage risks.

If our young bride and her GI had been lucky enough to buy a Levitt house in 1947, they would not have had a picket fence or ivy on the garden wall as she had hoped — Levitt's rules excluded fences and walls — and there would have been no fanlight over the door because their digs weren't quite that fancy. But they would have had a home they could afford, albeit with 4 ½ rooms and 800 square feet, more on the scale of an apartment and not quite all that dreams are made of (fig. 8). Levitt's house was, as *Harper's Magazine* then described it, the "Model-T equivalent of the rose-covered cottage,"[6] although *Architectural Forum* praised it as a "much better-than-average version of that darling of the depression decade — builder's Cape Cod" with proportions "considerably more pleasing than most of its variety."[7] While the Levitt house was small, the picture-book facade with its

8 Architectural rendering of one of the models of the Cape Cod houses built in Levittown, Long Island, in 1947. Nassau County Museum Collection, Long Island Studies Institute, Hempstead, New York.

40

clapboard siding and its shuttered windows recalled some elements of the dream, and it was good value, with an attic that could be readily finished to make an extra room and an enchanted kitchen decked out with all the appliances that one could need, even a washing machine, unprecedented in tract housing at that time.

Levittown's impact was immediate and widespread, as its successful formula for building houses and marketing them was featured widely in the national press. Large communities of shuttered Capes seemed to spring up everywhere in America's burgeoning suburbs as developers followed Levitt's lead almost by rote. But not two years later, Levitt, by then the nation's largest home builder, left its traditional dream house behind when, borrowing the annual model-change practice of the automobile industry, the firm introduced its 1949 model and it turned out to be modern (fig. 9; see detail fig. 5). Although the four thousand

houses built in Levittown that year retained the pitched roofs of the earlier Capes (to allow for the expansion attic), their centralized, shuttered facades were abandoned for a design that included a row of smaller striplike windows and an entranceway set back and to one side, and their interiors were thoroughly redone in a modern mode. Levitt's new open-plan model featured a living-dining-kitchen area divided by a red-brick wall complete with fireplace, a double-glazed picture window at back facing the garden where a patio and barbecue could be built (fig. 10), a row of the latest matching appliances, and clever built-ins. To someone accustomed to the boxlike layouts of typical prewar American homes with their discrete rooms, standard sash or casement windows, and decade-old appliances, Levittown was a vision of a new way of living that seemed to have transformed the future and brought it into the present for everyone.

10 Living room of a model house in Levittown, 1949, furnished in the Early American style and showing the picture window in the rear. Nassau County Museum Collection, Long Island Studies Institute, Hempstead, New York.

Levittown was the inspiration for the first novel set in a postwar tract-house community, *It's Only Temporary* by Charles Mergendahl, published in 1950, which even then described the conflicts of conformity and competitiveness that sociologists would soon discover in their own studies of suburban communities. Although the housing development in the novel is judiciously moved from Long Island to Westchester and called Campsville (after its fictional counterpart builder Edgar J. Camp), most of the features of the newly built houses, however caustically they are described, accurately match those of Levittown:

> There were ... many little keys (attractive features, he called them) that made "The House of Camp" the best buy, dollar for dollar, that could be obtained in the entire New York area, and possibly, as Mr. Camp often imagined, in the entire United States. Perhaps the most startling "attractive feature" was the living room. It was placed at the back of the house, "where living rooms belong," and the entire rear wall was one large picture window [see fig. 10]. There was a real, wood-burning fireplace, and a stairway that led upstairs to an unfinished second floor. (As Mr. Camp advertised, "You have the joy of finishing the second floor yourself.") One entered the house through the kitchen, a marvel of modern science, containing a range, refrigerator with deep freeze, a Bendix washing machine, and all-steel Lacy cabinets. These conveniences stood in a row on the left of the doorway. In the center of the inside wall was the bare chimney, with an opening some three feet above the floor, where one could barbecue over the open fire that was lighted in the living-room fireplace. There were two chambers — a master bedroom, measuring a big ten by eleven and a half, and a small room whose dimensions were eight by ten. ...
>
> All in all, the House of Camp was small, compact, and loaded with attractive features

found nowhere else but in expensive, custom-built estates. There were a few other features, however, that Mr. Camp failed to advertise. All the floors were linoleum-covered, all the walls were plywood, and all the lumber was green. Still and all, Mr. Camp had designed his town for "those nice young kids coming back from the war." ... And [it] had mushroomed with such incredible speed that now, in the spring of 1949, there were exactly four thousand two hundred and seventy-six of them. Outside they varied slightly. ... Inside they were precisely alike."[8]

The compact Levitt house indeed had many attractive features. It depended on the modern open interior arrangement and built-in equipment to maximize the square footage and make a logical entity of it. The firm, as one of the Levitt sons, Alfred, explained, "decided to borrow from Frank Lloyd Wright and put in a fireplace as the central pivot of the plan. We plotted circulation around the chimney, and

11   Advertisement for Jens Risom Design, *Interiors*, June 1949.

made the kitchen a control station from which the housewife [could] easily reach any part of the house"[9] as she took charge of its efficient management. A storage wall with louvered sliding doors was added to the tiny second bedroom so that a bureau would not have to take up floor space there. A second, movable and multipurpose unit, which served both as a guest closet and for dish storage or book-shelves, with a drop leaf that could be used as a desk or bar, stood next to the brick chimney between the kitchen and living room. For the detailing of this natural wood cabinet, Levitt had called on Jens Risom, a well-known designer, whose sophisticated modern furniture was reproduced frequently and advertised regularly in interior design magazines (fig. 11). Risom, who had emigrated from Denmark before the war, was one of only a few success-ful designers of modern furniture then active in New York. He had created the furnishings for the redwood "House of Ideas" that *Collier's* magazine built on a terrace in Rockefeller Center in 1940[10] and in 1941–42 designed the first line of furniture (light-wood cabinets, chests, bookcases, tables, and chairs with webbed upholstery) for Hans Knoll, who was just beginning to build the company that would become renowned in the 1950s as a manufacturer devoted exclusively to modern design.

Although the overall appearance of the Levitt houses was not aggressively modern (*Life* called it "semimodern"[11]), and would probably not have received FHA financing had it been so because most lenders thought the modern style was a fad that would not retain its value,[12] Levitt was the pioneer who introduced a number of significant modern features and the latest technology into tract housing, and in 1949 they

added a piece of Danish-style modern furniture
as well. New building features included open
floor plans and asymmetrical layouts (which
gave rise to the asymmetry seen on the
exterior), living rooms placed in the rear,
window walls, radiant heating in concrete-slab
floors, and storage walls. These were not
original with Levitt, having been developed
during the 1920s and 1930s and already used
in the construction of single houses and the
futuristic models showcased at such exhibitions
as the "Century of Progress" in Chicago in
1933–34 and the Town of Tomorrow at the
New York World's Fair in 1939. Many had also
been anticipated in *Tomorrow's House*, a book
written in 1945 by George Nelson, consultant,
and Henry Wright, managing editor, at
Architectural Forum, which brought together a
series of ideas for different aspects of modern
building. "The Colonial dream is approaching
its end," they predicted, "and the swing to
modern has definitely begun. All of our
tremendous apparatus for influencing public
opinion is tuning up for a new propaganda
barrage in favor of these new houses. A new
fashion in homes will be created, and the
public will follow"[13] — as they did in Levittown.
Conventionally associated with all that went
wrong with the suburbs (criticism appeared
almost immediately in the press and in fiction
such as Mergendahl's), Levittown has been
overlooked for its positive contributions, aside
from its considerable achievement of having
used mass-construction techniques to build tens
of thousands of units quickly for a nation very
much in need of affordable housing. For the
first time it also brought elements of modern
building to average homeowners in large
numbers, both directly and through the many
other housing developments that imitated the
innovations introduced in its successive yearly

models. "The $7,990 for which we sell our
house," Alfred Levitt noted in 1949 with the
pride of social commitment, "is a device by
which a few thoughts of the progressive
architects can be given to the public"[14] (even if
a number of the modern features were adopted
primarily because of their economic
advantages).

Levitt was not the only one to give modern
features to the public. In 1949 on the West
Coast, for example, Gregory Ain constructed a
community of one hundred flat-roofed houses
for families of average means,[15] and in 1952,
Cliff May transformed his expensive modern
ranch houses, which had evolved from the
informal California way of life, into reasonably
priced models.[16] Many local architects and
builders across the country were also choosing
from among such modern devices as flat roofs,
open plans, picture windows, and radiant
heating (which ultimately depended on the
designs of Frank Lloyd Wright) for the handful
of houses they were each constructing. But no
one else was to do it on such a large and
influential scale. In their own way Levitt's
pragmatic builder's structures can be compared
to the much-admired Case Study houses
sponsored by *Arts & Architecture* magazine,
which were designed in California by nine
noted architects, including Richard Neutra and
Charles Eames, beginning in 1945.[17] Levitt's
houses shared many of these same advanced
building features with the progressive Case
Study houses, conceived as prototypes of
affordable homes for professional and
intellectual families of moderate — not lower —
income. The Case Study program had
considerable architectural impact, particularly
on the West Coast and mainly on upscale
individual houses and developments, while for

their part, the Levitt houses had considerable building impact, introducing modern construction features to the mass market.

The GIs who lined up to purchase the houses in these new developments were truly a new breed of American home buyer; never before had families with little savings and limited incomes been in the position of owning their own dwellings. Young, somewhat broadened by their wartime experiences, and willing to work to maintain and improve their own homes (creating a postwar do-it-yourself craze that continues in America today), they were not restricted by the past and seemed to have been eager to experience what the future might bring. Certainly, the 37,000 people who in 1945 and 1946 sent unsolicited orders to reserve the factory-made "Wichita" houses designed by R. Buckminster Fuller[18] were free of conventional ties to what houses should look like, willing to invest considerably in a round futuristic house of tomorrow. Americans were caught up in a fascination with new possibilities in home building, and hundreds of thousands alone came to visit the Case Study houses in California, while across the continent every Sunday, families piled into their new cars and drove to the "country," waiting in line to trek through the latest in furnished model homes in anticipation of the day when they too could buy one and get to enjoy suburban living (fig. 12).

Choosing Modern

A bid for trade advertising for Mademoiselle's *Living* magazine in 1949 shows a young couple moving to their first house with the entirety of their possessions loaded in a single car. "They're saying good-bye to Mom ... and that's good for you," the advertisement reads. "Bag

and baggage, they're headed for home …
their own, their *first* home. And bag and
baggage is all they have! *As home furnishers,*
young Mr. & Mrs. are literally starting from
scratch."[19] Starting from scratch, they filled their
houses with new purchases, many of them
made possible with easy credit and with the
little additional money available because their
house payments were kept low through the GI
Bill. More and more, their purchases came from
the modern-style shopping centers that were
becoming the focus of suburban community
life,[20] and, with few possessions and few family
heirlooms that might induce them to choose
traditional styles, more and more their
purchases were modern.

They Came!
They Saw!
They Raved!
They Bought!

● *There is a National Home for
Every Home Buyer.*
● *Unsurpassed in Quality, Dura-
bility, Liveability, and Saleability.*

It will pay you to investigate the fine profit
possibilities that National Homes offers fran-
chised dealers. Write today for this information.

The presence of modern furniture on the postwar American market signaled a reversal of manufacturing trends in the country; during the war, in his book *Good-bye Mr. Chippendale,* the esteemed designer T. H. Robsjohn-Gibbings had decried its almost total unavailability. "Just how serious it is," he had explained, "was uncovered by the war emergency, when it suddenly became necessary to house millions of war workers. The housing schemes that were to accomplish this vast undertaking were in contemporary design and were well advanced when it was discovered that there was ... practically *no contemporary American furniture to be found.* The entire commercial furniture industry had become rotten to the very core by decades of reproducing the antique furniture of Europe and Colonial America, a fact which few people realized until the needs of war brought the grim facts into the open."[21]

Since the war, new firms had slowly begun to manufacture and import modern furniture, and modern lines were being added by some manufacturers of traditional furniture in order to tap into the emerging young home-furnishings market. Modern furniture and everyday objects were seen by the streams of visitors who attended the many exhibitions of design that were being organized in the United States. These were intended to bring the best products of good design, foreign as well as American, to the attention of consumers, enticing them with the prospect of goods that would soon become plentiful as normal production was re-established and encouraging manufacturers to make modern products available by demonstrating how much popular attention they would attract. In 1944 the Walker Art Center in Minneapolis initiated its Everyday Art Gallery,

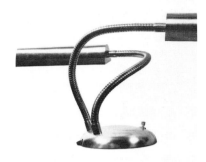

13   Cover of *Everyday Art Quarterly,* Fall 1949.

14   Model living room designed by Florence
Knoll (American) for "An Exhibition for Modern
Living" at the Detroit Institute of Arts, 1949.
Courtesy The Detroit Institute of Arts.

the first permanent space in the United States
devoted to the exhibition of modern utilitarian
objects, and promoted modern further by
publishing the best examples in its *Everyday Art
Quarterly* (later *Design Quarterly*), subtitled
A Guide to Well Designed Products (fig. 13). In
1948, the Buffalo (New York) Fine Arts
Academy presented "Good Design is Your
Business," which drew record crowds, and the
Akron (Ohio) Art Institute, "Useful Objects for
the Home," which had to be extended to
accommodate the large numbers who wanted
to see it.[22] This was Akron's fourth presentation
devoted to everyday objects and included
some two hundred products ranging in price
from twenty cents to twenty-five dollars. Taking
advantage of the institute's industrial design
testing laboratory, selections were judged with
regard not only "to design, but to the proper

use of materials, to operating efficiency and performance"[23] as well. In 1949 the Detroit Institute of Arts unveiled "An Exhibition for Modern Living," an enormous presentation organized with the support of the J. L. Hudson Company department store. It featured some three thousand "well-designed products" installed by the designer Alexander Girard and seven complete rooms furnished by different architects and designers (fig. 14).

The Museum of Modern Art in New York also mounted similar, though smaller, exhibitions of economically priced everyday objects during the 1940s, and it played an even more active role in influencing the direction of design by organizing several competitions, most notably, Organic Design in Home Furnishings in 1940 and the International Competition of Low-cost Furniture Design in 1948. These brought the results of new materials technology and design thinking directly to the marketplace through the association of the award-winners with cooperating manufacturers, and the work of many innovative figures — including Charles Eames and Eero Saarinen, the Italians Franco Albini and Marco Zanuso, and the British designer Robin Day — became known internationally through their participation in these competitions (and in the museum's exhibitions and publications that documented them). The goals of the low-cost design competition emphasized generally accepted postwar good design imperatives: "furniture that is adaptable to small apartments and houses, furniture that is well-designed yet moderate in price, that is comfortable but not bulky, and that can be easily moved, stored, and cared for; in other words mass-produced furniture that is planned and executed to fit the needs of modern living, production and merchandising."[24] The

52

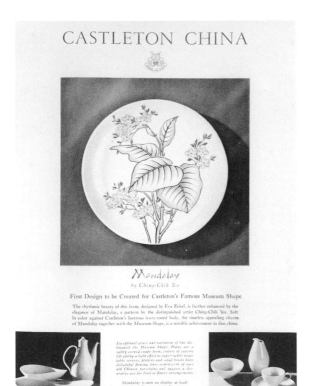

15 "Museum Shape" dinnerware designed by Eva Zeisel (American) with "Mandalay" pattern by Ching-Chih Yee, advertisement for Castleton China, *House and Garden*, November 1949.

museum's closest alliance with industry was its collaboration with Castleton China on a porcelain dinnerware service that became known as the "Museum Shape," which received much acclaim for its organic shapes when it was created in 1946 by the Hungarian-born American designer Eva Zeisel. But the ivory-colored service, issued without decoration in line with the museum's spare aesthetic vision, had limited commercial appeal, and the collaboration ran afoul when in 1949 Castleton began (without the museum's support) to market the service with various "extraneous" decorative patterns, the first being Ching-Chih Yee's floral "Mandalay" design (fig. 15).[25]

The most visible and far-reaching endeavor aimed at the marketing of modern design in keeping with this aesthetic was the series of "Good Design" exhibitions organized jointly by the Museum of Modern Art and the Merchandise Mart in Chicago between 1950 and 1955 and directed by Edgar Kaufmann, Jr. A venture that brought the museum into cooperation with large commercial interests, it represented a continuing commitment to influencing the course of contemporary design, not as the museum had done through competitions in the 1940s, when designers needed such encouragement, but by showing the work of such designers to aid manufacturers in making their products successful in the marketplace. The works were culled from a broad review of the manufacturing industries around the world (in 1953, for example, two

16   Advertisement for Konwiser, *Interiors*, December 1952.

54

hundred were chosen for the yearly exhibition in New York from a record of some eight thousand submitted, and considerably more were on view in the semi-annual showings in the large, commercial Merchandise Mart building in Chicago). The displays included furniture, tablewares, textiles, lighting, small appliances, and kitchen equipment. The works ranged from unusually innovative solutions for modern design problems to the merely clever, from works by the internationally famous to those by unknown designers, from the relatively expensive (regardless of the "Good Design" brief for economy) to the very cheap. "Good Design" brought considerable immediate prestige, especially in trade circles, and manufacturers were quick to take advantage of the inclusion of their products in the exhibitions as a stimulus for sales (fig. 16). The exhibitions served as the national arbiter in the field of modern design; because objects selected would be tagged in retail shops with "the LABEL that labels the products you sell as the best in modern design,"[26] retailers could rest assured that decisions of taste and quality had been made in an area of interior furnishings that may still have been uncertain to them. Through advertising, publicity, and merchandising (including mini-exhibitions in leading stores incorporating works from the shows), the impact of "Good Design" was extensive, and according to Kaufmann, the exhibitions helped "to decrease the disadvantages suffered by modern design, still subordinate as it is to imitative and bastardized wares which swamp the market quantitatively and dominate most promotional activity."[27]

In 1949 in an article entitled "Only in the U.S.A.," which presented the work of a cross-section of American designers, *House and*

Garden saw the energy and variety of modern design as emblematic of the American way (and an antidote to Iron Curtain totalitarianism, which was by then threatening the security of the West). "In a country which is a vast mélange of cultures and viewpoints," the article stated, "where everyone can say his say in words or wood or plastics or whatever he likes best, there is no single party line. Here we have the techniques to improve on life, hourly and daily, and the imagination and spirit to do new things constantly. These designers have one trait in common: they are the unmistakable product of a democracy. They have one object in common: to make American homes the envy of the world."[28]

America's homes were the envy of the world. In no other country did so many different types of people, including small business owners and blue-collar and office workers, have the opportunity to purchase their own new houses and to furnish them with the latest products, products that were, as one advertisement in 1949 oozed, "*charming as youth itself ... modern as this very moment ...* [and] priced for the moderate incomes of bright young moderns who want livable, lovable homes."[29] Even during the war when building permits were almost never issued and materials to carry out renovations were scarce, *Life, Look,* and other magazines ran feature stories about new building ideas and the use of plastics, plywoods, and other new technology, while home magazines brought an optimistic, upbeat viewpoint to articles about building, remodeling, and decorating in the modern style. "We like modern," wrote one participant in a survey of America's taste taken by *McCall's* at war's end; we "feel that this type of compact, streamlined house is designed 'special' for new war couples like us. Such houses are economical, built of fresh ideas, are a forward step in keeping with our demand for a brand new life in a brand new world." Exactly 33.4 percent of the participants preferred the modern house shown in the survey and even more of them liked modern design for specific types of furniture and interiors; 57.1 percent, for example, said they preferred the light, spacious, and adaptable contemporary living room that was one of the options the survey presented.[30] Many such couples were to follow these preferences when in the next few years they purchased new houses and furnished them in the modern style.

Popular Modern

While Charles Mergendahl did not pay much attention to the interiors of his fictionalized community Campsville (possibly because, as his title suggests, he could envision these streets of tract houses as only temporary havens from which his young couples were eager to flee), he did make several references to "sectional furniture" and "sturdy rock maple" — shorthand for the Modern and Early American decorating styles. Early American, a generic style with little decorative elaboration, had only vague connections to the colonial past and melded easily into these new interiors, a conservative alternative allied to Modern in the simplicity of its forms and materials (fig. 10). Not surprisingly, Modern and Early American were also the styles most often selected in the new suburban communities in the early 1950s,[31] while Modern, decisively reinforcing the image of the development,[32] was the style of 35 percent of the houses judged in a home-decorating contest in Levittown in 1952 (the others, as reported in *Life*, being 20 percent traditional and 45 percent an "eclectic mixture").[33] Maple and Modern were also chosen along with Traditional and Provincial as furnishings for the model houses in the Lakewood subdivision — dubbed "the city as new as tomorrow" — which opened near Long Beach, California, in 1950 (the first time a street of houses in various furnishing styles was used to encourage sales in a development).[34]

The Modern style that had quickly wedged itself into the lower-echelon home furnishing market comprised the most generalized of up-to-date elements, armless stuffed seating in rectangular or softly curving shapes (some, leftover adaptations of the late 1930s Moderne style) and rectangular cabinetry in light woods with simple metal or wooden handles, often set on splayed wooden legs, or on wiry metal ones, which could easily be attached with screws to give home-crafted furniture an updated look.

17   Bedroom suite, American, Sears, Roebuck and Co. catalogue, Fall/Winter 1951.

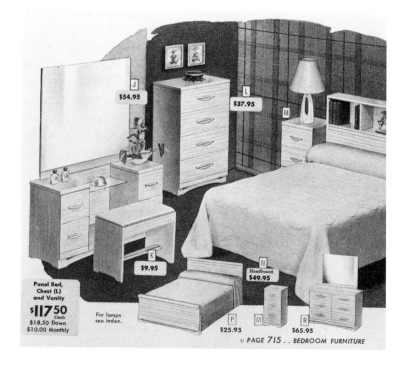

Floor-to-ceiling draperies, pole and tripod floor lamps and bold ceramic table lamps, shadow-box displays, and other newly designed accessories accompanied them. Such furnishings geared to the increasingly profitable market for inexpensive modern could be found at the large department and furniture stores that were opening in the suburbs, and could also be purchased from the national mail-order catalogues. By 1952 amid its pages displaying such traditional wares as Duncan Phyfe chairs, Sears Roebuck showed its Harmony House living room line offering "New! Exciting Modern Sectional Furniture" with "conventional modern arms" and "kidney shaped front" covered in "new nubby textured cotton and spun rayon boucle" or "wonderful, washable Vinyl-plastic."[35] Sears sold modern bedroom suites as well, including one in light gray oak veneer that was advertised as "ideal for 'young marrieds'" (fig. 17), once again emphasizing the youthful market for modern.

Grand Rapids Modern

With older and middle-class consumers, who were accustomed to the comforts of their period homes and traditional furnishings, the "swing to modern" that Henry Wright and George Nelson had predicted in *Tomorrow's House* was not so easily achieved. For those trying to convince this more affluent market to consider decorating in modern — first through magazines such as *Interiors* read by their decorators and retailers, and later, when it began to catch on in the early 1950s, through an increasing number of articles and advertisements in such high-circulation monthlies as *House Beautiful* and *House and Garden* — the effort to promote this style was limited only by the imaginative resources of the writers of editorial and advertising copy. For

59

those trying to take commercial advantage of this trend and appeal to the very decided tastes customarily satisfied with traditional furnishings from America's foremost furniture manufacturing center, Grand Rapids (Michigan) literally anything could be made to be modern if it was advertised that way — from the line of "perennial modern" molded birch-plywood furniture first created by the Finnish designer Alvar Aalto in the 1930s (fig. 18) to rattan sectional patio seating units called "Malay Modern" (fig. 19) to furniture in a vaguely late-eighteenth-century French style labeled "timeless modern" (fig. 20; the "modernity" of this table reinforced by its presentation in an up-to-date, free-form shape). For the most part, however, modern was still best defined in the negative, as anything that did not follow recognizable historical or traditional forms. But these too could partake of modern if, as an article in *House and Garden* entitled "Traditional Furniture with Modern Manners" indicated, they combined "period design and modern efficiency,"[36] such as furniture that was fitted out with double-duty elements.

The fact is that strict definitions were not the guiding principle in this market. For most Grand Rapids manufacturers and their customers, the modern style did not demand exclusivity within an interior, and, moreover, it was recognized that certain modern products melded well with a variety of decorating modes. The "Good Companions" exhibitions shown concurrently with the "Good Design" exhibitions at the Merchandise Mart in Chicago during the early 1950s displayed modern and traditional pieces side by side, aiming "to show that traditional and modern furnishings live well together"[37] and making sure that articles in the press about modern

18 "Perennial Modern," advertisement for Baldwin Kingrey, *Interiors*, December 1948.

19 "Malay Modern," advertisement for Ficks Reed, *Interiors*, June 1949.

design did not draw attention away from the more lucrative traditional furniture lines. A similar conflation of decorating styles is seen in a sketch of a bedroom in a 1951 advertisement for Widdicomb's Mid-Century Modern line (fig. 21), which from a bird's-eye view illustrates a Calder-like mobile, twin beds separated by a stepped night table, plain tapered lamps, free-form coffee table, and what look like French Provincial chairs — all creating what the *au courant* middle-class household would have seen as a modern interior. The venerable Widdicomb furniture company had been the first of the large commercial manufacturers in Grand Rapids to turn to modern when it hired T. H. Robsjohn-Gibbings in 1946 to create a modern production line and exploited his well-

20   "Timeless Modern," advertisement for Modernline, *Interiors*, December 1949.

21   "Mid-Century Modern," advertisement for John Widdicomb, *Interiors*, April 1951.

respected name to promote it. Robsjohn-Gibbings, a British-born designer brought to New York by the antiques dealer Charles Duveen, had achieved great success in the 1930s with the interiors he furnished and the custom classic furniture he designed for such famous clients as the tobacco heiress Doris Duke and the Dallas department store Neiman Marcus. In 1944, having decisively renounced his involvement and interest in antiques, he cajoled the readers of *Good-bye Mr. Chippendale* with the outspoken fervor of a reformed sinner into following his lead into the austere new world of modern. "Contemporary architectural thinking will point the way for you," he wrote:

> It will teach you to overcome the fear of empty spaces. All the meaningless prints, ornamental mirrors, whatnots, crystal candelabra and wall brackets used to fill empty spaces will go. Ornamental draperies, valances and fancy tie-backs will disappear. No more oriental rugs, homesick for mosques and bazaars, where their harsh-colored elaboration belongs. You won't even miss them when your eye becomes familiar with floors covered in one unbroken restful color running from room to room throughout the house. Your new furniture will be in a wood, the color and grain of which are left in their natural state. ... You will get a new pleasure from such woods, in contrast to the dark, stained, gloomy finishes of antique furniture. ...

> The new houses and their interiors are the new way of life of a new generation. They show a complete consciousness of today. They do not look to the past in envy nor to the future in wishful anticipation. They have come to perfect terms with the present. Wouldn't you enjoy the feeling that you are at one with the contemporary life that is the expression of this generation; that your house is tuned in to this moment in time; that you are glad to be living in the twentieth century — rather proud, in fact, to be a part of it? [38]

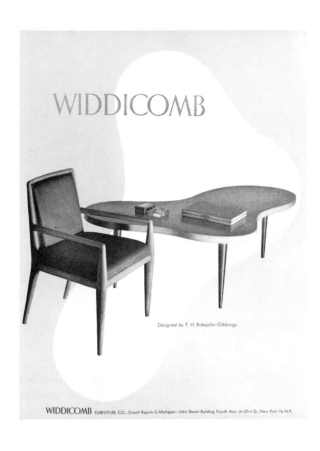

WIDDICOMB

Designed by T. H. Robsjohn-Gibbings

WIDDICOMB FURNITURE CO., Grand Rapids 2, Michigan—John Stuart Building, Fourth Ave. at 32nd St., New York 16, N.Y.

22   Armchair and coffee table designed by T. H. Robsjohn-Gibbings (American), advertisement for John Widdicomb, *Interiors*, February 1948.

Robsjohn-Gibbings's modern Widdicomb furniture, like that described in his book, was light-toned and elegant, with rounded tapering arms and legs (fig. 22), comfortable, stripped-down versions of the sophisticated designs that had made him famous in the 1930s; unlike that in his book, it was never threatening in its contemporaneity, and not nearly as austere as the style he described. His work seems to have appealed to the entire country; *Architectural Forum* reported in 1948 that Chicago's Marshall Field department store, "pace-setter for homemakers in the Midwest, has turned its impressive back on Chippendale in favor of the rather lavish contemporary pieces" of Robsjohn-Gibbings.[39] His work was successful

DUNBAR

for Modern

Easy Chair, heavy in scale, with open, leather-covered arms
and a fabric-covered seat and back. No. 4834

DUNBAR FURNITURE MANUFACTURING COMPANY | CHICAGO: 1438 MERCHANDISE MART
BERNE, INDIANA | NEW YORK: 227 EAST 56TH STREET
KANSAS CITY: 212 MERCHANDISE MART
BOSTON: 703 CLARENDON STREET

because it was market-driven. "People aren't
fools," he maintained. "In general, the public
taste is right and we must realize that modern
furniture must be designed on the public's
terms,"[40] which is just what he did. "For the
next ten years," *Interior Design* later recapped,
"magazines illustrated, householders purchased
and the furniture industry imitated the infinite
variety and classic serenity of the Robsjohn-
Gibbings designs."[41]

Widdicomb's move to modern "put fire in the
eye of period-minded Grand Rapids,"[42] as
Architectural Forum described it, and sent other
companies scrambling for modern designers.
By the beginning of 1950, more than half of the

23   Easy chair designed by Edward Wormley
(American), advertisement for Dunbar, *Interiors*,
November 1950.

American furniture industry had unveiled modern lines to supplement their regular production in traditional styles,[43] advertising them with such slogans as "Dunbar for Modern" (for the furniture of Edward Wormley, the firm's designer since 1931; fig. 23), "Definitive Modern" by Grosfeld House (for designs by William Breger and Stanley Salzman),[44] "Elegance in Modern" by Mason-Art (for furniture by Richard P. Lischer),[45] and "Baker Modern" (for the designs of the Danish architect Finn Juhl; color plate 2).[46] Like Widdicomb's modern, they were comfortable, easy-to-take designs, not extreme ones, and many retained subtle ties to the past and to traditional forms. These companies were hoping that the advice given by Robsjohn-Gibbings and by numerous magazine articles would spur America's middle class to spend money on redecorating their homes in the modern style and to choose modern furnishings when they moved into new apartments or to the more substantial houses that were being built for them in suburbia.

Good Design Modern

Not everyone in the decorating trade was behind the rush to modern. "Why are 90% of your editorial articles concerned with Modern," a reader of *Interiors* is quoted as asking in 1948, "when so large a proportion of your advertising is Traditional, and when so large a proportion of your readers believe in traditional styles?"[47] "If the interiors you advocate become the rule," another reader complained, "the vast majority of us will simply have to close shop. Drapery work-rooms do not stay open making up a wisp of nylon net to hang at one end of a thirty-foot expanse of plate glass; very few people feel that they need a decorator to tell them to put a pair of Eames chairs beside a

built-in sofa and a rubber plant in the corner."[48]
Speaking for its progressive readers throughout
America, the editor responded haughtily in
favor of modern, announcing that the
magazine was "published for those who have
made today's living possible, and are sweating
their brains out to make tomorrow's living
better."[49]

What these decorators took exception to was
not the elegant, inclusive modern furnishings
promoted by Grand Rapids that could easily be
used in conjunction with other decorating
modes but a modern that was spare and exclu-
sive, like the extreme good design aesthetic
Robsjohn-Gibbings had laid out for his readers
in 1944, when his enthusiasm for the new style
was at its height. Good design was self-
important and self-conscious, as conveyed by
the caption under an interior shown in an
advertisement in 1952, which asked: "Where
do you put radiators in a room this modern?"
(color plate 1). A typical good design interior
would have large picture windows and light
open interiors; floors of wood, stone, or
linoleum scattered with accent rugs or covered
with woven matting; foam-rubber cushions for
seating; fittings of plastic, plywood, or metal;
and abstract screen-prints or textured, woven
fabrics. It would more than likely boast a free-
form table by the sculptor Isamu Noguchi;
fiberglass or plywood chairs by Charles Eames
or Eero Saarinen or the imported Scandinavian
wooden furniture of Hans Wegner or Finn Juhl;
and storage systems by Eames, George
Nelson, or another successful young American
designer Paul McCobb. And as the reader
noted, a large potted plant would inevitably sit
in the corner. Indeed, with good design
interiors being so frequently illustrated in
magazines, their characteristic features were

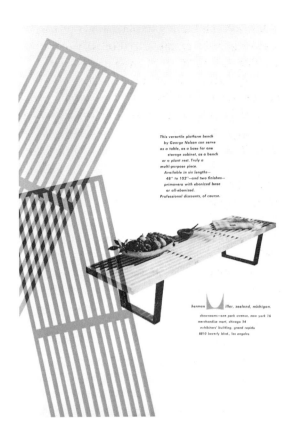

This versatile platform bench
by George Nelson can serve
as a table, as a base for one
storage cabinet, as a bench
or a plant rest. Truly a
multi-purpose piece.
Available in six lengths—
48" to 102"—and two finishes—
primavera with ebonized base
or all-ebonized.
Professional discounts, of course.

herman ller, zeeland, michigan.

showrooms—one park avenue, new york 16
merchandise mart, chicago 54
exhibitors' building, grand rapids
8810 beverly blvd., los angeles

readily copied, and they had a certain pul
repetitiveness that was picked out easily by the
reader, which immediately set them apart from
the others. For people cognizant of this type of
modern, they signified a precise level of taste,
sophistication, and intellectual appreciation.

Although such furnishings were quintessentially
modern according to anyone's definition, their
manufacturers and distributors, most conspicuously Knoll and its main competitor Herman
Miller, did not generally use the term "modern"
as a selling point in trade advertising. Modern
was what defined their lines, which featured
the most advanced design produced in the
United States and around the world, and

24   Platform bench designed by George
Nelson (American), advertisement for Herman
Miller, *Interiors*, March 1950.

presumably this would be understood by any professional reader. Instead, their modernity was emphasized by the sophistication of their advertisements, created by noted photographers and designers, where bold graphic invention meant more than mere photographic illustrations of their products (fig. 24). They did use "modern" in a popular context, however, and in one advertisement in *House Beautiful,* Herman Miller added the slogan, "Modern in the best sense of the word,"[50] implying a distinction between the firm's forward-looking original designs and the less adventuresome Grand Rapids creations, the popular inexpensive modern lines, and the numerous copies of their designs that could be had from a wide range of other manufacturers.

Despite the good design goal to make modern products economical, progressive work was often expensive, and by the early 1950s, a

25   Table designed by Isamu Noguchi (American), 1944. Ebonized birch and glass. Made by Herman Miller. The Museum of Modern Art, New York. Gift of Robert Gruen. (Copyright 1998 The Museum of Modern Art).

26 "Free form table designed by a famous artist," advertisement for Jan's Modern Lamps, *House Beautiful,* February 1955.

lively traffic in adaptations, copies, and imitations had emerged in the United States. Copying was continually a concern for Isamu Noguchi, whose distinctive designs repeatedly captured the eye of imitators. Noguchi's free-form glass-top coffee table (fig. 25), which he had created "in revenge" when a variation of the three-legged table he had designed for Robsjohn-Gibbings appeared in an advertisement under the latter's name, spawned numerous free adaptations as well as blatant copies. These were marketed widely, with one American retailer having the effrontery to advertise its pirated version in *House Beautiful* with the slogan "designed by a famous artist" (fig. 26). Noguchi's lamps too seemed to be fair game for imitators. "One day," he recalled, "somebody told me of a sign in a window, 'Noguchi-type Lamps.' The manufacturer, to whom I complained, said he had 'Calder-type' and 'Moore-type' lamps as well. If I didn't like mine, why didn't I design him one? When I devised what I thought was a contribution, all he could say was, 'Sorry, that's not a Noguchi-type lamp'."[51]

Similarly appearing in large numbers of copies was the casual "Butterfly" or "Sling" chair, created in 1938 by Bonet, Kurchan, and Ferrari-Hardoy (fig. 4, bottom). Constructed of a rudimentary welded-metal frame with a canvas or leather seat that slipped over it, this easy-to-fabricate chair became one of the best sellers of the 1950s. It was distributed internationally by Knoll in an authorized version with a canvas or leather seat (see fig. 14), but was also copied extensively by craftsmen in their own home workshops and by numerous small manufacturers, much to Knoll's chagrin. The chairs seemed to be everywhere, and were advertised for sale cheaply through magazines and mail-order catalogues. In the July 1952 issue of *House and Garden* alone, three different advertisements offered the chairs at heavily cut-rate prices (fig. 27).

If one accepted the principle of universal accessibility that had been the goal of

27 "Sling" chair, advertisement for Today's House, *House and Garden*, July 1952.

progressive design for a century and was espoused by so many designers in the 1950s, copying (if it was done well) should have been welcome, a sign that all their proselytizing for modern design had paid off. But *Interiors,* reporting in 1954 that many of the selections chosen for the "Good Design" exhibitions had been "boldly, if not always successfully, copied by frankly commercial manufacturers,"[52] thoroughly disapproved of this practice. The extensive copying of Finn Juhl's Danish-style furniture for Baker after it was published in beautiful, measured, colored drawings in *Interiors* in 1951 (color plate 2) was for Lazette Van Houten, writing in *Arts & Architecture,* a "notorious example of how fast less-talented designers and manufacturers can be converted to new design theories," although she did admit "it is none the less true that such thievery has resulted in a broader conception of design by more manufacturers and in many cases in better design for persons unable to afford the original."[53] In a picture spread in the *New York Times Magazine* in 1953, Betty Pepis, home furnishings editor, showed a number of original modern designs, from Italian lamps and furniture by Hans Wegner to abstract textiles by Alexander Girard, side by side with copies of them (some almost exact replicas). She suggested that "the system, which has long been accepted in the fashion field, has certain obvious advantages for the home consumer — better design at budget prices (although the price decrease is sometimes gradual). Not only the actual copies, but the competition offered by the copies creates awareness of the importance of 'design' by the manufacturer of less expensive items,"[54] and eventually the greater availability of modern design to greater numbers of people. By mid-decade, when modern designs had become successful and modern clichés were seen everywhere, the question of copying was being reconsidered within the industry, as an editorial in *Interiors* made clear:

> The field of interior design is not a total chaos in which each designer goes his way with absolute independence. But neither are the designers (or the public) as complete sheep as in the fashion industry. The less creative designers imitate the more creative, but there is considerable variety in what the more creative are doing, and so the public has a choice. ... Each season sees not a single trend but many, with advents of new Eames types, new Finn Juhl types, new Mies types, and so on. It is inevitable and not necessarily deplorable that these imitative processes should take place. The line between "inspiration" and theft is hard to draw, but wherever it belongs, true originality is hardly common. Not only that, but it is far from indispensable to a good design performance. Unless we are sure that the influenced or "inspired" designer is a conscious plagiarist, we should evaluate his performance in terms of line, proportion, and other design elements rather than in terms of originality.[55]

Modern Abroad

Amidst the devastation of the war and the efforts of recovery, modern design abroad took considerably longer to come into its own than in the United States, and when it did, it was free from the ambivalence of definition that widespread American marketing and advertising to many different groups of consumers had created. Government social welfare policies recognized the relevance and economic advantages of spare, efficient design as a means of rebuilding quickly and bringing equity to living standards. But even in Great Britain, where promoting modern along the principles of good design was government policy, modern never had the broad backing that American manufacturers gave it, nor the hefty encouragement of the popular press that would make the switch to modern an easy decorating choice.

The severe restrictions placed on British manufactures at the outbreak of the war had affected virtually all consumer products, and all furniture had been made according to the strict regulations of the government's Utility program (introduced in 1943), leaving little room for independent design of any type. In order to preserve vital resources, Utility had prescribed the materials that could be used in essential manufactures, the designs that could be made, and even the colors that could be employed for fabrics. The program drew on the craft values that had been revived by the British Arts and Crafts movement in the later nineteenth century, leavened by a pinch of European modernism (which had not otherwise been widely accepted in Britain), to create a line of simple, anonymous furnishings, sturdy and well made, that were modern in feeling. Although the designer Gordon Russell, who had been head of the Utility design panel and later director of the Council of Industrial Design, claimed success for Utility as a means of introducing good design and raising "the whole standard of furniture for the mass of the people ... giving them something better than they might be expected to demand,"[56] it did not seem to change the preference of the public for traditional styles. According to one retailer writing in 1949 to *Design*, the Council's magazine, "as soon as the regulations were relaxed and manufacturers were offering reproduction styles, most of the Utility designs, good though they were, were practically unsaleable."[57]

Good design had been the controlling factor in the design conception presented at the "Britain Can Make It" exhibition in London in 1946, a vast showcase anticipating the revitalization of British industry and a didactic display meant to teach modern design principles to the public.[58] Organized by the Council of Industrial Design, which had been founded in 1944 for the purpose of stimulating the sale of British manufactures, "Britain Can Make It" was presented at the Victoria and Albert Museum in London, where, twice extended, it was seen by almost a million and a half visitors. Modern principles also guided design at the Festival of Britain, a major celebratory exhibition held in 1951. With exhibits confined "to contemporary production, contemporary techniques and the contemporary idiom in design,"[59] the Festival's emphasis was on "the present." For the first time, the millions of visitors to the Festival of Britain were confronted with a completely modern environment. Architecture, interiors, displays of household products and industrial design, graphics, and even souvenirs were all coordinated by the Council. What visitors saw as they strolled through the fairgrounds on London's South Bank was a thrilling array of modern structures, awkwardly synthesizing engineering and architectural innovations, bright, upbeat furnishings, and consumer products that, although sharing an international modern vocabulary, gave Britain a confident push along a broad path of independent contemporary design.

Britain had never been comfortable with the spare decorating style that modernism had introduced there in the 1930s, especially in light of its long history as an international pacesetter of ornamental design. As early as 1949, an article in *Design* had complained that "the cult of the plain surface has gone much further than the demands originally made by functionalists and labour-savers,"[60] and that same year, an editorial in the magazine called for "More Pattern and Colour." This was the opportunity, it said, "to launch a new tradition of pattern and colour in the decorative arts and the craft-based industries. We are not asking for rococo cookers or baroque adding machines, but we join with our critics when they suggest that there is something wrong with a generation which prefers the pallid to the robust and the anaemic to the full-blooded."[61] One effort toward finding new inspirations for the revival of pattern — the curious idea of taking the varied organic and geometric shapes that define the structures of crystals as the source for a unifying design concept for the Festival of Britain — was already under way. "I had it in mind that we are at a stage in the history of industrial design," wrote its proponent Mark Hartland Thomas, then chief industrial officer of the Council of Industrial Design, "when both the public and leading designers have a feeling for more richness in style and decoration, but are somewhat at a loss for inspiration. Traditional patterns that have come down to us from ancient Greece and elsewhere, had lost much of their sparkle by now; and the fashionable alternative of a doodle on a piece of paper, folded for symmetry, could hardly lay the foundations of a new school of design."[62] Thus Hartland Thomas brought together twenty-six manufacturers of textiles (fig. 59), pottery, lace, plastic laminates, ceramics, and other such products to experiment with the use of crystallography as the basis for ornamental design at the Festival and for products meant for export. Called the "Festival Pattern," this was heralded at that time as a distinctive new approach to ornament, melding the discoveries of science with the creativity of art. Whether it really provided "that new subject matter which is sometimes held to be a precondition of the revival of ornament" was questioned by the *Architectural Review*,[63] but on a large and very visible scale, the short-lived Festival Pattern did introduce the public to abstract surface patterning, which would become extremely popular in Great Britain in fabrics and wallpapers throughout the decade.

It was no accident that the Festival of Britain followed good design principles, for the government was banking on using its experience with the Utility program to improve the standard of living of a large segment of the population and the design and quality of goods manufactured for export, which were vital to Britain's economic development. The government promoted a type of conservative modern design for the housing blocks and new towns being built for workers, and across the entire social fabric through industrial design exhibitions and educational programs, such as *Design* magazine (founded in 1949). This was a large-scale effort. The Council of Industrial Design worked to convince British industry that "Good Design Is Good Business" (fig. 28), and it could show the furniture of Ernest Race (including his "BA" chair designed in 1945 and made of scrap wartime aluminum [fig. 29] and the wiry "Antelope" and "Springbok" chairs used throughout the Festival of Britain), Robin Day's modular wooden storage and seating units made by Hille, and the textiles of Lucienne Day (notably her abstract, plantlike "Calyx" design, a gold medal winner at the Milan Triennale in 1951) as examples of success stories in the field of modern design. To encourage the public to choose modern, the press, particularly the popular women's

28 "Good Design is Good Business," advertisement for Dolcis, from *Design in the Festival* (1951).

magazines, published suggestions for the economical furnishing of basic apartment units, and exhibitions such as the annual Ideal Home Show in London also presented new ideas and products for modern interiors, with the result that organic and Scandinavian-inspired wooden furniture gained a considerable popularity. Television also played a part in promoting modern, with the BBC choosing objects from lists of approved modern furnishings drawn up by the Council of Industrial Design to decorate the sets of television dramas and public affairs programs.[64]

In the Scandinavian countries, where the legacy of the English Arts and Crafts movement was long lasting and influenced the continued growth of the craft industries, the arrival of an accessible modern design was evolutionary, with the greatest headway having probably been made in the 1930s, and not in the 1940s and 1950s.[65] Scandinavian modern furniture was cautious, most of it handmade of natural materials and often drawing inspiration from traditional forms, like that of Hans Wegner,

which had Chinese (color plate 9), English vernacular, and American Shaker antecedents. The glass and ceramics industries, which had taken major steps toward the introduction of modern design early in the century, created both well-conceived utilitarian lines (fig. 30) and decorative objects, which, confident in their wedding of craft and production, could explore a wide variety of ornamental treatments. What was seen abroad as evidence of a new, modern spirit in design — when Scandinavian products took numerous prizes at the Triennale exhibitions in Milan in 1951 and 1954 and when they were first exported in large numbers to the rest of Europe and to America after the war — had come about slowly. If the quality and quantity of these exports made it seem to those abroad that every Scandinavian home was furnished with such simple decorative and comfortable utilitarian modern designs, this was only a small part of what was being offered for sale there (and elsewhere in the world), with the remainder being traditional in style and not always of the highest quality.[66]

In Italy, more than anywhere else abroad during the early postwar period, an entire population had direct involvement with progressive design in their daily lives — at work, on the street, in bars — because of the mass distribution of a number of industrial products that were conceived in a distinctively modern, expressive style, including Vespa scooters made by Piaggio (from 1946), Gio Ponti's round, gleaming espresso machine designed for La Pavoni (1948–49), and Marcello Nizzoli's organic "Lexicon" typewriter for Olivetti (1948), and the easy adoption of eccentric modern styling for the decoration and furnishing of commercial interiors. An initial

30   "Kilta" dinnerware designed by Kaj Franck (Finnish), 1952. Glazed earthenware. Made by Arabia. Courtesy Wärtsilä Ab Arabia, Helsinki.

push by architect designers to utilize modern standardization and design as the means of bringing adequate housing and products to everyone had little lasting impact. The government's social policy lost its energy and the endeavors of individual designers and corporations took responsibility for a new design that was both more technologically inventive and more stylish. Italy's craft-based industries allowed for the rapid introduction of new ideas that explored the organic vocabulary, new materials (such as foam rubber, sheet and tubular metal, plastic, and plywood), and flexible solutions for them — but their products were destined for high-end buyers at home and for export worldwide (although small crafts shops could quickly create their own versions of these designs as required for popular consumption). Italy's place as a significant force in postwar modern was pressed through the Triennale design exhibitions in Milan and its sleek design magazines such as *Domus* and *Stile Industria,* and solidified in 1954, when the Milanese department store La Rinascente presented its first national design prizes, the Compasso d'Oro (Golden Compass), which gained substantial international prestige.

Most of the furnishings produced during the early period of recovery in West Germany were steeped in the security of past and vernacular styles. Modern design reappeared only slowly, much of it along the lines of Germany's prewar attachment to the severity of functionalist form, which had been most publicized through the products and teachings of the Bauhaus design school and the activities of the German Werkbund. This was underscored in 1955 with the opening of the Hochschule für Gestaltung (Institute of Design) in Ulm, the "spiritual" successor of the Bauhaus,

which had been closed by the Nazi government in 1933. But there was also a separate
craftlike involvement in the expressive organic
vocabulary of modern with the independent
artistic exploration of biomorphic forms in
furniture (color plate 10) and ceramics.[67] While
progressive manufacturers such as the metalware firm of Carl Pott and the Rosenthal
porcelain company espoused the aesthetic of
good design, the export market on which they
relied did not consistently support this. The
distinctive modern shapes of Raymond Loewy's
organic "Exquisit" porcelain dinnerware (1953)
and his hourglass "Form 2000" service
(designed with Richard Latham; 1954), both
commissioned by Rosenthal and known best
today in examples with little or no decoration,
depended on ornamentation for most of their
sales and were advertised and sold successfully
over the next decade in 23 and 165 different

abstract, biomorphic, and pictorial patterns respectively (fig. 31). Rosenthal's high-end Studio Line, inaugurated in 1954 with the awareness that it was decoration that would ultimately bring the appreciation of modern design to a large affluent market,[68] issued products created by well-known international artists, architects, and designers that combined both modern forms and abstract and representational decoration (fig. 32).

Modern design emerged even more slowly in Japan, where it drew on both the residue of direct, prewar contacts with the philosophy of the Bauhaus and the fallout of occupation, when even the scraps of American culture were admired and interpreted by young Japanese designers trying to come to terms with the future.[69] It openly expressed admiration for Western models and depended almost totally on the concept of good design (fig. 33), learned through cultural interchanges, a philosophy that also worked easily with Japanese sensibilities and allowed for the emergence of a modern design that related to Japan's own traditions (fig. 34). For the Japanese public, however, modern seemed to arrive almost in a flash, at the moment when Toshiba's electric rice cooker (fig. 35) appeared on the market. In a country with relatively few possessions still bound to age-old methods, the cooker was accepted by virtually all Japanese women; it totally altered their outlook as a shiny metal and plastic appliance invaded their traditional homes and reduced the time and effort needed to prepare the daily meals, paving the way for the introduction of a succession of other such modern products.

In France, the movement to bring economical modern design to the public through such

exhibitions as the "Formes Utiles" (Useful Forms) series, first presented by the Union des Artistes Modernes in 1949, had relatively little impact on a broader acceptance of design by the public. Based on prewar modernist ideas about the value of utilitarian and standardized everyday objects dominated by the commanding image of Le Corbusier, these exhibitions included works mostly by designers who had come to prominence before the war, among them Charlotte Perriand and Jean Prouvé. Nor did proposals by other designers for a more distinctly French modern style, for example, the attenuated furniture forms, decorative grid structures, and witty lighting designs postulated by Jean Royère (color plate 3), garner much popular success. Most French

36 The New Look "Bar" suit designed by Christian Dior (French), Spring 1947. (Copyright Association Willy Maywald – ADAGP).

37   Cover of *Art & Décoration*, number 29, 1952. Illustrated is part of an interior designed by Jacques Dumond for the Salon des Décorateurs, Paris.

ART &
NUMÉRO **29**
DÉCORATION

revue fondée en 1897
LIBRAIRIE CENTRALE DES BEAUX-ARTS

designers were reluctant to turn their back on the traditions of craftsmanship and luxury that for several centuries had set the country apart as a leader of style and design. This was true even of Christian Dior's celebrated New Look, unveiled in 1947 (fig. 36). While Dior's approach to women's fashion may have been "new" and closely allied formally to the contemporary use of hourglass and tulip shapes in design,[70] conceptually the New Look was not modern. Twice regressive, it looked back to the nineteenth century in its lines and in the profligacy of its construction, introducing a superfluity of fabric at a time when material goods were still in short supply, as well as an abundance of enrichment, such as embroidery and sequins, when progressive design required an aesthetic of spare and economic functionality.[71] When French craftsmen, some belonging to the same prestigious firms that had exhibited their Art Deco cabinetry, lighting, and textiles at the 1925 Paris exhibition, did explore the forms of the new international design, they often produced works of such stylish refinement that they seem like parodies of economy-minded modernity (fig. 37).

1   *Life*, January 22, 1945, inside front cover.
2   Raymond Loewy, "What of the Promised Post-War World — Is It Just a Dream, Or Will It Come True?," *The New York Times Magazine*, September 26, 1943, p. 14.
3   See Stephen W. Sears, *The American Heritage History of the Automobile in America* (New York: American Heritage Publishing Co., 1977), pp. 279–81.
4   An early series of articles on the "prefabrication movement in America" was published in *Architectural Forum* beginning in December 1942 and continuing through 1943; see also Gwendolyn Wright, *Building the Dream: A Social History of Housing in America* (New York: Pantheon Books, 1981), pp. 244–46.
5   "Fuller House," *Life*, April 1, 1946, p. 73.
6   Eric Larrabee, "The Six Thousand Houses that Levitt Built," *Harper's Magazine*, vol. 197 (September 1948), p. 82.
7   "4,000 Houses Per Year," *Architectural Forum*, vol. 90 (April 1949), p. 85.
8   Charles Mergendahl, *It's Only Temporary* (Garden City, N.Y.: Doubleday & Company, 1950), pp. 8–9.
9   Quoted in "4,000 Houses," cited above, p. 86.
10 See Edward Durell Stone, *The Evolution of an Architect* (New York:

Horizon Press, 1962), p. 94.

11 "Levitt Adds 1950 Model to His Line," *Life*, May 22, 1950, p. 142.

12 See Wright, *Building the Dream*, cited above, p. 251.

13 George Nelson and Henry Wright, *Tomorrow's House: How to Plan Your Post-War Home Now* (New York: Simon and Schuster, 1945), p. 6.

14 "4,000 Houses," cited above, p. 86.

15 See "One of a Hundred," *Arts & Architecture*, vol. 66 (September 1949), pp. 40–41.

16 "Fast Selling California Ranch Houses by Cliff May," *House & Home*, vol. 2 (October 1952), pp. 90–91.

17 See Esther McCoy and others, *Blueprints for Modern Living: History and Legacy of the Case Study Houses* (Los Angeles: The Museum of Contemporary Art, 1989).

18 Martin Pawley, *Buckminster Fuller* (London: Trefoil Publications, 1990), p. 107.

19 Advertisement, *Interiors*, vol. 108 (June 1949), p. 45.

20 See Geoffrey Baker and Bruno Funaro, *Shopping Centers: Design and Operation* (New York: Reinhold Publishing Corporation, 1951).

21 T. H. Robsjohn-Gibbings, *Good-bye Mr. Chippendale* (New York: Alfred A. Knopf, 1944), p. 6.

22 As reported in *Interiors*, vol. 107 (February 1948), p. 16.

23 Akron Art Institute, *Useful Objects for the Home: A National Survey and Exhibition, Presenting a Guide to Well Designed Objects for Everyday Use* (November 2-December 2, 1947), n.p.

24 Edgar Kaufmann, Jr., *Prize Designs for Modern Furniture from the International Competition for Low-cost Furniture Design* (New York: The Museum of Modern Art, 1950), p. 6.

25 The *Everyday Art Quarterly* (no. 14 [Spring 1950], p. 6), similarly committed to modernist design, lamented "the one-step-forward-two-steps-backward which have been taken by Castleton; this ware is also being manufactured with applied patterns designed by prominent artists, one of whom remarked that he felt that the familiar cliché 'gilding the lily' was unusually apt in this case."

26 Advertisement, *Interiors*, vol. 111 (September 1951), p. 30.

27 Edgar Kaufmann, Jr., "Good Design '51," *Interiors*, vol. 110 (March 1951), p. 100.

28 "Only in the U.S.A.," *House and Garden*, vol. 96 (July 1949), p. 28.

29 Advertisement, *House and Garden*, vol. 95 (January 1949), p. 22.

30 See Mary Davis Gillies, "Mr. and Mrs. McCall Know What They Want," in the "Home Omnibus" issue of *Architectural Forum*, vol. 82 (April 1945), pp. 101–8, quoted from p. 102.

31 Based on an informal survey reported by Harry Henderson in "The Mass-Produced Suburbs: I. How People Live in America's Newest Towns," *Harper's Magazine*, vol. 207 (November 1953), p. 26.

32 Herbert J. Gans noted in *The Levittowners: Ways of Life and Politics in a New Suburban Community* (New York: Pantheon Books, 1967), p. 270, that "fifty-four per cent [of the residents] had shifted from modern to traditional" when they moved to the Levittown community built in New Jersey in 1958. "The principal impetus was the pseudo-Colonial façade of the Levitt house, and 70 per cent of those changing to traditional furniture chose 'Early American'." One resident's comment, "If the house had been Oriental, we would have bought bamboo," shows how influential the stylistic choices of Levitt and other builders were on popularizing furnishing styles in the period.

33 "Same Rooms, Varied Decor," *Life*, January 14, 1952, p. 90.

34 See D. J. Waldie, *Holy Land: A Suburban Memoir* (New York: W. W. Norton & Company, 1996), pp. 35, 37.

35 Sears, Roebuck and Co., *Catalogue*, Fall/Winter 1952, pp. 744–45.

36 "Traditional Furniture with Modern Manners," *House and Garden*, vol. 95 (March 1949), p. 113.

37 Hortense Herman, "Side by Side — Modern and Traditional," *Retailing Daily*, April 27, 1951, illustrated in Terence Riley and Edward Eigen, "Between the Museum and the Marketplace: Selling Good Design," in *The Museum of Modern Art at Mid-Century: At Home and Abroad* (New York: The Museum of Modern Art, 1994), p. 173.

38 Robsjohn-Gibbings, *Good-bye Mr. Chippendale,* cited above, pp. 104–6.

39 "Marshall Field Rooms," *Architectural Forum,* vol. 88 (January 1948), p. 13.

40 Quoted in "Grand Rapids Modern," *Time,* January 30, 1950, pp. 51–52.

41 "Robsjohn-Gibbings: 25 Years of His Work," *Interior Design,* vol. 32 (May 1961), p. 123.

42 "Three New Furniture Lines," *Architectural Forum,* vol. 86 (January 1947), p. 116.

43 "Grand Rapids Modern," *Time,* cited above, p. 51.

44 Advertisement, *Interiors,* vol. 112 (May 1953), p. 11.

45 Advertisement, *Interiors,* vol. 109 (March 1950), p. 57.

46 Advertisement, *Interiors,* vol. 111 (April 1952), p. 186.

47 Quoted in F. de N. S., "Merry Christmas!!," *Interiors,* vol. 107 (February 1948), p. 75.

48 Quoted in George Nelson, "Problems of Design: Modern Decoration," *Interiors,* vol. 109 (November 1949), p. 69.

49 F. de N. S., "Merry Christmas!!," cited above, p. 75.

50 Advertisement, *House Beautiful,* vol. 95 (March 1953), p. 82.

51 Isamu Noguchi, *A Sculptor's World* (London: Thames and Hudson, 1967), p. 26.

52 "Good Design: The Fifth Anniversary Show," *Interiors,* vol. 114 (August 1954), p. 82.

53 Lazette Van Houten, "Five Years of Good Design," *Arts & Architecture,* vol. 71 (June 1954), p. 34.

54 Betty Pepis, "When Designs Are Copied," *New York Times Magazine,* November 29, 1953, p. 52.

55 "Riding the Currents," *Interiors,* vol. 115 (May 1956), p. 73.

56 Gordon Russell, *Designer's Trade* (London: G. Allen and Unwin, 1968), p. 200.

57 J. W. Wright, Letter to the Editor, *Design,* no. 10 (October 1949), p. 25.

58 See Penny Sparke, ed., *Did Britain Make It?: British Design in Context 1946–86* (London: The Design Council, 1986).

59 P. R., "Industry and the 1951 Festival," *Design,* no. 2 (February 1949), p. 1.

60 Noel Carrington, "Decoration in Contemporary Industrial Design," *Design,* no. 5 (May 1949), p. 2.

61 P. R., "Wanted: More Pattern and Colour," *Design,* no. 9 (September 1949), p. 1.

62 Mark Hartland Thomas, "Festival Pattern Group," *Design,* nos. 29–30 (May–June, 1951), p. 14.

63 *Architectural Review,* vol. 109 (April 1951), p. 236.

64 The government's programs are nicely reviewed in Catherine McDermott, "Popular Taste and the Campaign for Contemporary Design in the 1950s," in Sparke, ed., *Did Britain Make It?,* cited above, pp. 156–64.

65 See, for example, Gunilla Frick, "Radical Change or Stagnation?: Swedish Post-War Decorative Art," *Journal of Scandinavian Design History,* vol. 6 (1996), pp. 43–53.

66 See Jean Stewart, "Selling Design in Sweden," *Design,* no. 2 (February 1949), pp. 11–12.

67 See Horst Makus, *Der Alltag der Moderne: Die Keramik der Aera Adenauer* (Stuttgart: Arnoldsche, forthcoming).

68 See Philip Rosenthal, "Design for Market," in Kathryn B. Hiesinger and George H. Marcus, eds., *Design Since 1945* (Philadelphia: Philadelphia Museum of Art, 1983), pp. 27–30.

69 See the recollections of the graphic designer Yusaku Kamekura, quoted in Kathryn B. Hiesinger and Felice Fischer, *Japanese Design: A Survey Since 1950* (Philadelphia: Philadelphia Museum of Art, 1995), p. 15.

70 See Lesley Jackson, *The New Look: Design in the Fifties* (London: Thames and Hudson, 1991).

71 These themes were discussed by Richard Martin and Anne Alter at a session entitled "The 50th Anniversary of the Dior 'New Look'," Fashion History Association, February 12, 1997, at the College Art Association, New York.

raymor

Of special interest to
Dealers, Decorators and
Architects, Raymor
presents — America's
most comprehensive
collection of
contemporary lamps,
both functional and
decorative, created by
eminent designers . . .
plus an important group
of coffee and end tables,
and modern decorative
accessories of unusual
distinction . . . also,
the Chronopak Clocks
designed by
George Nelson.
All are now on display in
our enlarged showrooms
. . . or write Dept. N2 on
professional letterhead
for your copy of
the Raymor catalog.

Which Modern?

"'Modern' isn't enough!" the readers of *Interiors* learned from an advertisement in 1952. "No longer is it a question of 'modern or traditional.' More often, the customer will ask, 'Which modern?'"[1] Recognizing the efforts made to promote modern and the strides taken since the war toward its wider acceptance in the United States (as well as the increasing popularity of modern abroad as other nations were pressing the economics of production as part of their recovery), the advertisement confirmed that modern had made it. It also recognized that modern came in many different forms, which by the early 1950s had become so varied and so individualistic that any attempt to force them into a single style would have been futile (fig. 38).

In an article on modern furniture written as the 1950s were beginning, George Nelson tried to provide some structure for understanding it. As an editor, author of numerous articles and books, and designer himself, Nelson took a sensible approach to design as a matter of problem solving, which had perhaps the greatest impact on American design thinking during the immediate postwar period. He identified three distinct "influences" on modern design — what he called the "machine look," the "handicraft look," and the "biomorphic look."[2] Using these rubrics (which, as he explained, had to do solely with the appearance of objects and not with their methods of manufacture), he was able to establish useful, albeit imprecise and often overlapping, categories that embraced the major tendencies that had already been clearly established in so many designs of the late 1930s and 1940s and which would continue to describe design throughout the decade.

38   Advertisement for Raymor, *Interiors*, February 1950.

The Machine Look

The machine look, he wrote, was meant "to dramatize machine forms and emphasize the role of the machine in modern life." A well-defined, geometric version of this style had been the beacon of modernism before the war, its stripped-down aesthetic and use of industrial materials symbolizing to the previous generation the mechanistic imperative of life in the twentieth century. This style of functionalist architecture and design had belonged very much to the sophisticated world of the avant garde; it evolved in Europe early in the century in the work of such International Style architects as Walter Gropius, Le Corbusier, and Ludwig Mies van der Rohe. Most characteristic of the style were its glass, metal, and reinforced-concrete buildings as well as the metal furniture (fig. 4, top row), lamps, unornamented ceramics, and other housewares made to furnish them during the 1920s. Especially influential were the industrial prototypes for consumer goods created at the Bauhaus design school in Dessau, Germany. The machine look

39 "T" chair designed by Katavolos-Littell-Kelley (American), 1952. Chromed steel and leather. Made by Laverne International. Philadelphia Museum of Art. Gift of Carl L. Steele.

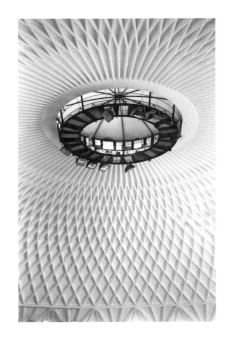

also included many products of streamlining: the shiny, aerodynamic creations of the new breed of American industrial designers such as Henry Dreyfuss and Raymond Loewy — although partisan distinctions in the United States separated them from the more rigorous, geometric, functionalist aesthetic that had been promoted from the early 1930s under the aegis of the Museum of Modern Art in New York.

The machine look of the 1950s can be interpreted much more broadly. It was not limited to the smart, sleek machine imagery that had been inherited from such works as the "Barcelona" chair, designed by Mies van der Rohe in 1929 (fig. 4, top left), which along with its matching stool and table were the only examples of prewar functionalist metal furniture sold in America during the 1950s. It was also not limited to the imagery that was being reinterpreted in such designs as Katavolos-Littell-Kelley's three-legged "T" chair of 1952, which played on the functionalist vocabulary of chrome and leather (fig. 39). The look embraced more complicated structures and newer technologies, materials, and forms. Thus, to the architectural geometry of glass and steel and the curving lines of bent tubular-metal furniture were added the highly individualistic expression of engineering and intuition. Examples of this could be seen in the reinforced-concrete exhibition halls, sports stadiums (fig. 40), and transportation centers designed by the Italian engineer Pier Luigi Nervi and the prefabricated industrial components of the Case Study house of Charles Eames, with its exposed strut supports (fig. 41), repeated in the base of his fiberglass chair (frontispiece), and in his modular storage system (color plate 4). The additive effect of Eames's work was echoed in Achille and

40 Dome of the Palazetto dello Sport, Rome, designed by Pier Luigi Nervi (Italian) and Annibale Vitellozzi (Italian), 1956–57.

CASE STUDY HOUSE FOR 1949

Arts & Architecture's case study house
for 1949 is truly a study of logical use
of materials and integration of spaces.
Materials long used in common practice, by the very directness of their application here, take on a new fresh-
ness. The results will be provocative
to many and, for all we know, might
be one of the small steps toward the
development of a building idiom for
our time.

THE BLACKSTONE CORPORATION
ALTEC LANSING CORPORATION
KIERULFF AND COMPANY
AMERICAN STOVE COMPANY
BERGER KITCHEN CABINETS
REPUBLIC STEEL CORPORATION
CANNON ELECTRIC DEVELOPMENT COMPANY
MINNEAPOLIS-HONEYWELL REGULATOR COMPANY
W. A. CASE & SONS MANUFACTURING COMPANY, INC.
GOODYEAR TIRE & RUBBER COMPANY, INC.
AMERICAN CABINET HARDWARE CORPORATION
KLEARFLAX LINEN LOOMS, INC.
KNAPE & VOGT MANUFACTURING COMPANY
CHICOPEE MANUFACTURING SPECIALTIES CO.
MODERN BUILDING CORPORATION
UNITED STATES PLYWOOD CORPORATION
C. W. STOCKWELL COMPANY
SWEDLOW PLASTICS COMPANY
THE PAYNE FURNACE CORPORATION
GOTHAM LIGHTING CORPORATION
GRANT PULLEY & HARDWARE COMPANY
MEILINK STEEL SAFE COMPANY
E. L. BRUCE COMPANY
DEERLING MILLIKEN & COMPANY, INC
THE FORMICA COMPANY
CENTURY LIGHTING, INC.
BOLTA PRODUCTS SALES, INC.
MISSISSIPPI GLASS COMPANY
PRYNE & COMPANY, INC.
TRUSCON STEEL CORPORATION
THE CELOTEX CORPORATION
THE SUNBEAM CORPORATION

★ merit specified the case study house program of the magazine

Piergiacomo Castiglioni's *ad hoc* "Luminator"
floor lamp made of undisguised industrial
elements, steel tubing, steel tripod legs, and a
bare flood lamp (fig. 42). The machine look
was equally expressed in the refined creations
of sophisticated factory production, such as the
round glass "Fuga" bowls designed by the
Swede Sven Palmquist for manufacture by
centrifugal force (fig. 43) and the enameled
"Krenit" bowls by the Dane Herbert Krenchel,
which were made of cold-pressed millimeter-
thin steel plate (color plate 6). But it was also
presented literally in the referential propeller-
like electric table fan by Ezio Pirali (fig. 44) and
conceptually, through the precision and the
sophisticated interplay of coloration in the
geometrical "Pythagoras" fabric by the Swede
Sven Markelius (color plate 5).

41   Promotion for the Case Study House of
1949 designed by Charles Eames, *Art &
Architecture*, April 1949.

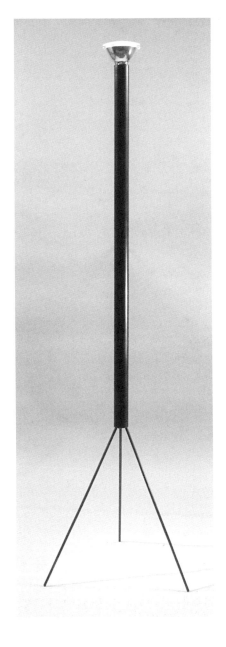

42   "Luminator" floor lamp designed by Achille Castiglioni (Italian) and Piergiacomo Castiglioni (Italian), 1955. Steel. Made by Gilardi e Barzaghi. Montreal Museum of Decorative Arts. The Liliane & David M. Stewart Collection.

43   "Fuga" bowls designed by Sven Palmquist (Swedish), 1950. Centrifugally cast glass. Made by Orrefors. Courtesy Orrefors Glasbruk, Orrefors, Sweden.

44   Table fan designed by Ezio Pirali (Italian), 1954. Metal and rubber housing. Made by Zerowatt. Courtesy Zerowatt S.p.A., Bergamo.

The Handicraft Look

The handicraft look, "that easy, rounded look
that spells home and comfort," was a dominant
and an accessible component of modern design
in the early 1950s. Because works that shared
in the handicraft aesthetic used familiar, natural
materials such as wood, clay, and wicker, and
conveyed a sense of informality, they seemed to
have a more immediate appeal to average
consumers who were taking bold enough steps
in furnishing their new houses with modern
design that they saw the handicraft look as a
means of adding warmth, comfort, and a sense
of security to their homes. The look had been
out of fashion for several decades, however,
superseded by a preference for the high polish
and crisp decorative embellishments of period
reproductions, the cold, utilitarian finish of
metal and glass in the works of European
machine-look modernism, and the sleek curves
and aerodynamic lines of the streamlined
Thirties, regardless of whether the objects were
made by hand or machine.[3] This contradictory
approach, in which handcrafted works were
made to look like machined objects, had been
apparent during the 1920s in many of the
products of the Bauhaus. To achieve an
anonymous, machined look, for example, many
hours of handwork had been spent on metal
and glass lamps made in the school's workshops, very much to the amusement of out-
siders. The designer Wilhelm Wagenfeld
described the reaction of manufacturers at a
trade fair who "laughed over our products.
Although they looked like cheap machine
products, they were in fact expensive handi-
crafts."[4]

Valuing the qualities of immediacy and
imprecision that are customarily associated with

45 "Superleggera" chair designed by Gio Ponti (Italian), 1952–57. Ash and cane. Made by Cassina. Philadelphia Museum of Art. Gift of Atelier International, Ltd.

handmade objects is an aesthetic concept that dates in the West to Victorian England. It came as a reaction to ruthless industrialization voiced by the most famous English critic of art and architecture of the period, John Ruskin. His dislike of the repetitive perfection of machine-made objects, his emphasis on the human values of handwork, and the communitarian elements of his social beliefs were adopted by William Morris and his followers in the Arts and Crafts movement in Great Britain, the United States, and Scandinavia around the turn of the century. These designers found their metiers in the crafts, deliberately allowing the traces of their hand workmanship to remain visible as they followed standard age-old craft processes and revived others that had been lost during the long period dominated by the machine. Sometimes they also reinterpreted the handicraft forms of earlier periods, as Morris did in the creation of his rush-seated "Sussex" chairs of the 1860s, based on a type of British country seating, which became one of the best selling lines of his firm Morris & Company. During the 1950s, the Italian architect and designer Gio Ponti followed a similar path when he turned to a nineteenth-century Italian vernacular form as the model for his light, attenuated, cane-seated "Superleggera" chair (fig. 45); for several years he labored to create a classic modern design but one that evoked the handcraftsmanship of what he called the "true 'traditional chair'."[5] A number of his compatriots, including Franco Albini and Roberto Mango, also found in traditional crafts, particularly wicker work, a medium in which to express modern design.

The handicraft aesthetic remained a strong element in other works of modern design that evolved from the forms of traditional cultural life across the globe, even as they partook of limited series or advanced factory-production techniques. This was seen in Japan in the textured *shizuku* (dripping water) mold-blown glass of Masakichi Awashima (fig. 46); in Italy at the furnaces of Murano, where throughout the decade, artisans created individualized designs in series, such as the distinctive, colored vessels of Fulvio Bianconi, particularly those made with his pieced *(vetro pezzato)* mosaic-like technique (color plate 7); and in the United States, where hand weaving was adapted for the decorative window blinds designed by Dorothy Liebes in combinations of unorthodox materials, including bamboo, ribbons, chenille, metallic threads, grasses, and beads (color plate 8).

The handicraft look included most of the products of Scandinavian design that were propelled to international popularity in the early 1950s — oiled wooden furniture (color plate 9) that recalled traditional hand working and finishing methods (even if it was often made in large part by machine); ceramics with painted and molded decoration; unique examples of blown glass; as well as hand-printed textiles — all of which emphasized the inherent nature of their materials and techniques and the accidental or unique elements in their manufacture. Combined with this was a new appreciation of the craft objects made elsewhere, such as the thin, delicately turned wooden bowls by the American James Prestini (fig. 47) and the quiet forms of studio potters, including the work of Hans Coper, Bernard Leach, and Lucie Rie in Great Britain and Getrud and Otto Natzler in the United States (fig. 48). The handmade look also spread through commercial ceramics, where the accidental effects esteemed by these

94

46   Drinking glass designed by Masakichi Awashima (Japanese), 1955. Blown and cast *shizuku* glass. Made by Awashima Glass. Philadelphia Museum of Art. Gift of Mrs. Masakichi Awashima.

47   Bowl designed and made by James Prestini (American), 1945. Mahogany. Philadelphia Museum of Art. Gift of the designer.

48   Bowl designed and made by Gertrud Natzler (American) and Otto Natzler (American), 1946. Glazed earthenware. Philadelphia Museum of Art. The Louis E. Stern Collection.

49   Flower holders designed by Russel Wright (American), 1945. Made by Bauer Pottery. Collection of Steven Beyer, Penn Valley, Pennsylvania.

50   "Kanttarelli" (Chantarelle) vase designed by Tapio Wirkkala (Finnish), 1947. Blown and etched glass. Philadelphia Museum of Art. Gift of COLLAB: The Contemporary Design Group for the Philadelphia Museum of Art.

artisans were exploited in roughly shaped, unglazed vessels as well as in the loose applications of thick, brightly colored glazes. The attempt by the well-known American designer Russel Wright to imitate effects of handmade and studio pottery in large-scale machine production runs for the Bauer Pottery Company (fig. 49) failed, however, because of technical problems and lack of consumer interest.

The Biomorphic Look

For Nelson, the biomorphic look, which used "biological, or organic form," was "neither homey like the handicraft object nor rigid like the machine form but amorphous and flowing like living tissue." Nelson's prime example was the furniture of the American sculptor Isamu Noguchi. Nelson illustrated two free-form coffee tables, one with three legs and one with a demountable, interlocking base (fig. 25), and a sinuous, elongated sofa, all manufactured by Herman Miller. But biomorphism, which includes the exuberant asymmetrical shapes so closely associated with the Fifties, was much broader (color plate 12). It could be sophisticated and subtle, like the engraved, paper-thin "Kantirelli" vases created by the foremost

Finnish designer and craftsman Tapio Wirkkala
(fig. 50) and the innovative stainless-steel
"Design 1" cutlery by Don Wallance (fig. 51);
plainly utilitarian, like Russel Wright's mottled
melamine "Residential" table service (fig. 52);
or whimsical, like Ben Rose's hand-printed
"Hole in Stocking" fabric (fig. 53). But most
characteristic was the emblematic, boomerang
shape, which was adapted ubiquitously for
furniture, such as the mosaic coffee table
designed by the German Ruth Richter Hesse
around 1952 (color plate 10) and the diminutive
chair-side snack tables produced in great
numbers for sale in Britain in the early 1950s
(fig. 54). The aerodynamic boomerang was a
shape used frequently in textiles — in the
popular colors of red, yellow, lime, aqua, gray,
and pink — often in combination with stylized
plantlike motifs (color plate 11), and in plastic
laminates, most famously, the "Skylark" pattern
created for Formica in 1951 by Brook Stevens
Associates (fig. 55). A fluid organicism also
extended to the design of appliances — not the
rounding corners of Thirties streamlining but the
flowing sculptural shapes made possible by the

51   "Design 1" cutlery designed by Don
Wallance (American), 1954. Stainless steel.
Made by C. Hugo Pott. Philadelphia Museum of
Art. Gift of C. Hugo Pott.

52   "Residential" serving dish designed by
Russel Wright, 1953. Melamine. Made by
Northern Industrial Chemical Company.
Author's collection.

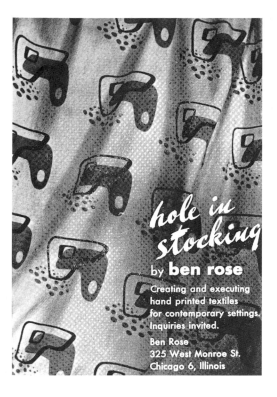

53 "Hole in Stocking" fabric designed by Ben Rose (American), advertisement for Ben Rose, *Interiors,* November 1946.

54 Snack table, British, *c.* 1950–55. Wood. Author's collection.

55 "Skylark" and "Fernglo" patterns designed by Brook Stevens Associates (American), advertisement for Formica, *Interiors,* April 1951.

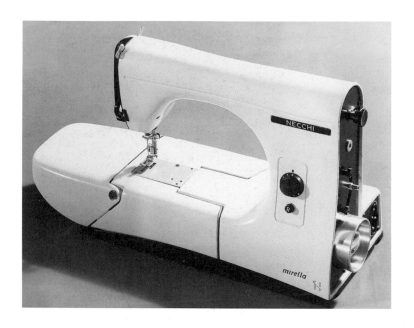

new plastics technology, such as Marcello
Nizzoli's sewing machine for Necchi (fig. 56).

Biomorphic shapes, which brought a totally
new formal language to the creation of
common, utilitarian objects, can be clearly
related to European artistic developments of the
1920s and 1930s, notably the soft, amoeboid
forms found in the dream world of the Surrealist
artists, particularly in the works of Jean Arp
(fig. 57), Salvador Dali, and Joan Miró. Free-
form and organic shapes were also introduced
in design during the 1930s, in the undulating
glass vases of Alvar Aalto (fig. 58) and in such
unusual pieces of furniture as the nested
aluminum coffee tables created by the
Romanian-born American architect Frederick
Kiesler.[6] The postwar period had a kind of
residual familiarity with biomorphic design,
which did not simply derive from paintings,
reliefs, objects and its appearance in avant-
garde advertising and graphics. It also came

56   "Mirella" sewing machine designed by
Marcello Nizzoli (Italian), 1956. Enameled-
aluminum housing. Made by Necchi. Courtesy
Necchi S.p.A., Milan.

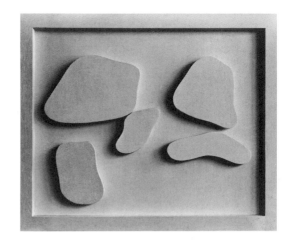

57 *Constellation* by Jean Arp (French), 1932. Painted wood relief. Philadelphia Museum of Art. The Louise and Walter Arensberg Collection.

58 Vase designed by Alvar Aalto (Finnish), 1936. Glass. Made by Karhula-Iittala. Philadelphia Museum of Art. Gift of Design Research.

59 "Surrey" fabric designed by Marianne Straub (British), 1950. Wool, cotton, and rayon. Made by Warner.

from the flat, multi-colored, irregular painted and printed wartime camouflage patterns (known especially from the photographic coverage of the Pacific campaign) that were closely related to them. This uncanny resemblance was not lost on the writer of a 1944 article on the aesthetics of landscape camouflage, who questioned the determinism of such shapes: "Can there be any rational explanation," he asked in the caption under a work by Miró, "of the striking similarity of camouflage patterns to this 'painting-poem' …? Is it possible to assume that artists of another age would have devised other camouflage shapes and believed in them?"[7] The biomorphic amoeboid form was also confirmed in nature on a submicroscopic level with the structural diagrams used as models for a number of the Festival Pattern designs, such as Marianne Straub's "Surrey" furnishing fabric (fig. 59). Earlier design sources for biomorphic forms are also known, although a path of direct inspiration from them to designers in the 1950s cannot be charted. Among them are the "kidney table" (fig. 60), published in Thomas Sheraton's *Cabinet-Maker and Upholsterer's Drawing-Book* (1791–94), given its name "on account of its resemblance to that intestine part of animals so called";[8] and the gently undulating quatrefoil tops of American spool-legged parlor tables from the late Victorian period (fig. 61).[9] With such a variety of antecedents Fifties design could claim as original only some of the sinuous free-, trilo-bate-, kidney-, palette-, and boomerang-shapes that appeared so regularly during the period both as flat decorative patterning and for the forms of such diverse objects as serving plates, ashtrays, tables, countertops, and even swimming pools, regardless of the decorative style in which they were presented (fig. 62).

Biomorphism invited comparisons between design objects and animal and humanoid shapes. The ceramic salt and pepper shakers created around 1946 by Eva Zeisel for her "Town and Country" dinner service (fig. 63; see color plate 12)) suggest a psychological

60   "A Kidney Table" designed by Thomas Sheraton, plate from *The Cabinet-Maker and Upholsterer's Drawing-Book*, 1791–94 (London, 1802). Philadelphia Museum of Art Library.

61   Table, American, c. 1880–90. Wood. Author's collection.

62   Advertisement for New Era, *Interiors*, June 1950.

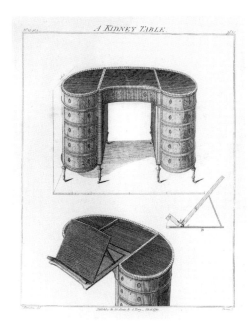

relationship between the two pieces, be it
human or animal. This was noticed by one
writer, who commented that the shakers took
"affectionate, confiding attitudes no matter how
they [were] placed on a table" and reported
that the "first critics to see them thought they
looked like mother and baby seals, while others
compared them to a human family."[10] Something of this close relationship was paralleled in
the conjoined "Lazybones" salt and pepper
shakers (fig. 64), designed for the Frankoma
Pottery by its founder John Frank, while Zeisel's
warmly evocative forms were also compared to
Shmoos,[11] the highly engaging organic-shaped
beings in Al Capp's comic strip *Li'l Abner*. Their
selflessness in becoming whatever was needed
for the country's satisfaction and economic well-
being, be it a pound of butter or a sirloin steak,
captivated America in 1948 and inspired a host
of fad products, from deodorizers, clocks, and
planters to toys and rattles (fig. 65).[12] Similar
humanoid associations inspired the perception
of Henning Koppel's eccentric hand-wrought
silver water jugs as "pregnant" (fig. 66) and
brought the names "Womb" to Eero Saarinen's
deep, enveloping, upholstered-fiberglass easy
chair (fig. 67) and "Lady" to a chair by the

Italian designer Marco Zanuso, which was part of a seating series described in an American advertisement as "anthropomorphism in foam" (fig. 68).

To visualize the connection between design and biomorphic form that he outlined in his article in 1949, Nelson published a provocative montage of elements taken from many different furniture designs and shown in silhouette (fig. 69) as if they had been wrenched out of the paintings of Joan Miró (fig. 70), Arshile Gorky, or Jean Arp or dismembered from the sculptures of Henry Moore, Alexander Calder, or Isamu Noguchi. For the readers who might not understand the point Nelson was making with the silhouette montage, the caption made it very clear: "The forms produced by the

63 "Town and Country" salt and pepper shakers designed by Eva Zeisel (American), c. 1946. Glazed ceramic. Made by Red Wing Pottery. Collection of Steven Beyer, Penn Valley, Pennsylvania.

64 "Lazybones" salt and pepper shakers designed by John Frank (American), 1946–53. Glazed ceramic. Made by Frankoma Pottery. Author's collection.

65 Plastic toy in the shape of a Shmoo, American, c. 1949. Afterglow Antiques, Shoreham, Vermont.

66 Wine jug designed by Henning Koppel (Danish), 1948. Silver. Made by Georg Jensen. Kunstindustrimuseet, Copenhagen.

67 "Womb" chair designed by Eero Saarinen (American), 1946. Plastic, chromed steel, and upholstered latex foam. Made by Knoll. Courtesy Knoll, Inc.

68 "Zanuso's Anthropomorphism in Foam," advertisement for Altamira, *Interiors*, July 1955.

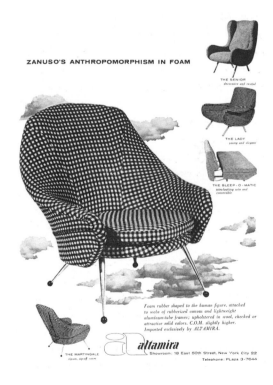

ZANUSO'S ANTHROPOMORPHISM IN FOAM

The forms produced by the furniture designer show that he is subject to the same influences as the artist, for they are less related to function, technique, materials, production, etc., than to

furniture designer show that he is subject to the same influences as the artist, for they are less related to function, technique, materials, production, etc., than to modern painting and sculpture."[13] This startling assertion, which was totally at odds with the functionalist insistence on utility that for over a century had been voiced as a determining factor in progressive design, demonstrated that by the close of the 1940s, aesthetics — or, as the catalogue of the New York "Good Design" exhibitions stated, "eye-appeal" — now came first.[14]

In another article, "The Contemporary Domestic Interior," published in *Interiors* a year later, Nelson reinforced this approach to the creation of form. He analyzed the conception of the modern house with its large windows, room dividers, storage systems, and free-standing

69   Illustration from "Modern Furniture" by George Nelson, *Interiors*, July 1949.

70   *Painting* by Joan Miró (Spanish), 1933. Oil and aqueous medium on canvas. Philadelphia Museum of Art. A. E. Gallatin Collection.

fireplaces, and suggested that "because of the new problems presented, all sorts of objects are re-examined and then redesigned so that they can stand clear of all walls, whether opaque or transparent. At which point, of course, they become sculpture. The fact that you may still sit in some of them, as in Eero Saarinen's big chair [fig. 67], or park your drinks on others, such as the Noguchi [fig. 25] or [William] Armbruster coffee tables, is relatively inconsequential. Regardless of their ultimate use, these objects are designed as sculpture is designed."[15] Paul McCobb, designer of economical modern furniture groups sold successfully through department stores, agreed. ("A chair," he explained, "is seen from all angles, like a piece of sculpture. It should be light and open, to increase the feeling of scale — and the psychological effect of more space

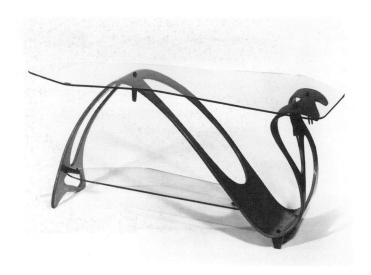

in the room.")[16] Saarinen also concurred, seeing the problem of his design of objects with structural shells, "a sculptural one."[17]

The sculptural approach was most apparent in designs with the biomorphic look, particularly those created in Italy, by Nizzoli, Zanuso, and the Turinese architect Carlo Mollino, whose severely bent and pierced plywood tables (fig. 71) were obviously influenced by modern sculpture like that of Moore. The one-piece Ericofon telephones introduced in Sweden in 1956 were described by the Swedish design journal *Form* as "technical sculptures … [which] more clearly than anything else, depict the art of our age" (fig. 72).[18] The most astonishing assessment of design as sculpture, however, appeared in 1954 in the American magazine *Industrial Design,* which was moved to profess that the deeply modeled organic form of Gio Ponti's toilet designed for Ideal Standard (fig. 73) "suggests that of the Winged Victory of Samothrace."[19] The sculptural approach was not restricted to furniture, household objects,

71   Tea table designed by Carlo Mollino (Italian), *c.* 1950. Maple-faced plywood, brass, and glass. Made by Apelli & Varesio. The Brooklyn Museum. Gift of the Italian Government.

72   Cover of *Ericsson Review,* 1956, introducing the Ericofon telephone.

73   Toilet designed by Gio Ponti (Italian), 1953. Vitreous china. Made by Ideal Standard. Philadelphia Museum of Art. Gift of Ideal Standard.

and appliances; fashion designers using corsets and padding took to molding the body into literal organic sculptures (fig. 36), while architecture was also being transformed into monumental, biomorphic forms. This was perhaps explored most daringly by Eero Saarinen in his tense, aquiline TWA airline terminal building at Idlewild (now Kennedy) Airport in New York (1956–62) and, most potently, by Le Corbusier in his mystical pilgrimage chapel at Ronchamp in France (1951–55; fig. 74).

Art and Design, Design and Art

If by the beginning of the 1950s design had become sculpture, then industrial designers had become artists. This was a signal leap from their role as salesmen and cosmeticians in the 1930s, when they streamlined the products of industry to meet competition in the market-place, and as social activists following the war, when in line with the good design brief, many directed their efforts toward raising the level of housing and making good, economical products available to a large segment of the population. In creating the curriculum of the new design school in Ulm, Max Bill, a Bauhaus-trained Swiss sculptor, announced that its founders "believe art to be the highest expression of human life and their aim is therefore to help in turning life itself into a work of art"[20] — a heady prospect even for designer-artists. The new artistic status of the designer was suggested by the increasing use of designers' names with their manufactured products, which added cachet to these works and glamour to the world of home furnishings. The passion of some historians to redistribute these works and attach the names of office associates to products that were ascribed solely to the designers during their lifetimes, most notably George Nelson and Charles Eames, can easily distort today's understanding of the fame and position that these designers held during the 1950s and diminish appreciation of them as the generators of creative ideas. The remembrances that John and Marilyn Neuhart had of working in Charles Eames's office, which "appeared to run on democratic principles but was in fact a kind of monarchy [where] all projects began and ended with Charles,"[21] calls into question, for example, the spirit of the revisionist practice of attributing

74   Notre Dame du Haut, Ronchamp, France, designed by Le Corbusier (French), 1951–55.

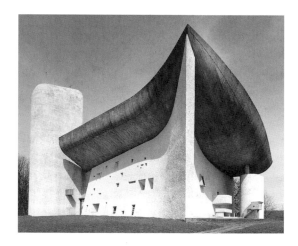

Eames's work collaboratively to his wife Ray (and sometimes to the other associates in their office).

This new status of design was solidified in 1954 when the Milan Triennale chose as one of the themes of its tenth international exhibition, the collaboration of the world of art with that of industrial production;[22] the same year, La Rinascente established the prestigious Compasso d'Oro (Golden Compass) design awards with the criterion for excellence based on "the aesthetic of the product."[23] This emphasis on aesthetics was underscored semantically by the use of "industrial aesthetic" as a term for design in Italian and French, and by the French periodical *Esthétique Industrielle* (founded in 1950 by Jacques Viénot), which discussed objects of design in terms allied to those used for the criticism of art.

As designers were being elevated to artists, sculptors and painters were becoming designers. Noguchi, as we have seen, had been a significant force in design since the mid-1940s, with his biomorphic chairs, sofas, and tables — particularly his coffee table with its reversed, segmented base (fig. 25), which *Art News* considered an extraordinarily successful translation of "abstract art into applied art."[24] Max Bill created an entire range of machine-look furniture and rigorously functionalist clocks and lighting, and the American Harry Bertoia, trained as an artist in metal, produced a series of open-work, steel-wire-shell chairs for Knoll (some of which were partially or fully uphol-stered; fig. 75). These he equated with sculp-tural "studies in space, form, and metal. ... If you will look at these chairs," he said, "you will find that they are mostly made of air, just like sculpture. Space passes right through them."[25]

75   "Diamond" chair designed by Harry Bertoia (American), 1952. Steel and upholstery. Made by Knoll.

In their own work, many artists also crossed over, further clouding the distinction between the arts and the crafts. Italian sculptor Lucio Fontana, for example, worked with a direct craftlike involvement in polychrome majolica during the early postwar period, and his compatriot sculptors Mirko and Afro also explored this craft medium. The most famous, and most influential, cross-over effort was that of Picasso. Working at the Madoura pottery in the traditional ceramic center of Vallauris in the south of France beginning in 1947, he was responsible for a continual outpouring of energetic designs that were translated into editioned works. When his ceramics were shown at the Triennale in Milan in 1951, Gio Ponti — like George Nelson an influential editor (of the magazine *Domus*) as well as a designer and architect — announced that the "Picasso episode" made France "dominant in the world of ceramics."[26] It brought attention back to local pottery centers and their lively forms and decoration, which were frequently based on folk techniques and imagery. The immediacy of Picasso's figures and animals painted on and incised into ceramics made them especially prized, and they were never far from commercial exploitation as replica (fig. 76) or by association (as in the "Picasso-esque Pottery" from Vallauris highlighted in *House and Garden* in 1952[27]).

Painters were also a frequent source for design, especially for textile and wallpaper patterns. Characteristic motifs were adopted, for example, by the celebrated artists Alexander Calder, Matta, Henri Matisse, and Joan Miró for the large "mural scrolls" they created for the Katzenbach and Warren wallpaper firm in New York in 1948. Such motifs also appeared in the designs by Marc Chagall, Raoul Dufy,

76 "Replicas of Picasso's Ceramic Plates," advertisement for Perspectives, *Interiors*, January 1950.

Fernand Léger, Miró (fig. 77), and Picasso that
inspired the Modern Master Print series of the
American textile manufacturer D. B. Fuller in
1955–56, used both as furnishing fabrics and
for apparel. Young abstract artists also lent
their vision to printed fabrics, including those
that the CoBrA painter Karel Appel designed in
1953 for 't Paapje in the Netherlands and that
Fontana created for the Manufattura Jsa in Italy
in 1954–55. Three New York Abstract
Expressionist painters, William Baziotes,
Adolph Gottlieb, and Robert Motherwell, also
supplied designs for printed fabrics,
commissioned in 1950 by the Onondaga Silk
Company.[28] Both Surrealist and abstract in their
imagery, the designs by these and other
modern artists in a vast array of contemporary
styles,[29] were a tangible means of bringing
modern artistic ideas directly to the public, who
could now curtain their windows with fabrics
by Matisse and shop for dresses tagged "A
Modern Master. Designed by Léger."[30]

Modern abstract art was also becoming more
visible in the public sphere as a result of the
many commissions that placed sculpture (most
significantly, that of Alexander Calder, Jacques
Lipschitz, and Henry Moore) as well as large-
scale architectural decoration in paint, ceramic
tile, mosaic, stained glass, and sculptural relief
throughout Europe and America. These
included, for example, a huge colorful abstract
mosaic created by the Italian painter Giovanni
Dova for the facade of a Milan apartment
building designed by Marco Zanuso in 1951
and a geometric tile decoration by Herbert
Beyer for Walter Gropius's Harvard University
Graduate Center of 1949–50.[31] A prominent
early postwar expression of public confidence
in decorative abstraction was the commission
given to the Bauhaus-trained sculptor Amerigo

Tot for the colossal, monochromatic steel frieze in relief that runs across the facade of the central railroad station built in Rome in 1951 (fig. 78), with a repeating pattern of subtle linear activity that brings to mind the interplay of boomerang and biomorphic forms on contemporary textiles, wallpapers, and laminates.

The relevance of artistic expression to everyday activity was the theme of the exhibition "Modern Art in Your Life" held at the Museum of Modern Art in New York in 1949. "The forms of modern art are part of modern living," the catalogue proclaimed. "This directly contradicts the point of view that the modern artist is isolated from the rest of the world, and his work therefore without meaning for his fellow men." But "the artist has given form to a vision which the designer then makes his own, and indeed the designer often frankly follows after the artist, adapting to his own uses the latter's invention and discovery."[32] To Max Bill, writing in his book *Form: A Balance Sheet of Mid-Twentieth-Century Trends in Design*, the designer had little choice. "Designers who realise new forms," he explained, "are

78   Steel relief (detail) designed by Amerigo Tot (Italian), 1951, for the facade of the Stazione Termini, Rome.

consciously or unconsciously reacting to trends in contemporary art because it is in art that the intellectual and spiritual currents of every epoch find their visible expression. Works of art may often be ridiculed or misunderstood when first produced but their almost immediate influence on every branch of design soon becomes apparent."[33] Those who understood modern art only in terms of subjective, individualistic expression, however, made a clear distinction between such works designed by "recognized non-commercial artists" and those produced by others. "The influence of living artists on interior decoration has been immense," the art historian James Thrall Soby acknowledged, "but very often it has been forced by other hands through commercial filters which have taken the good out of it — and the taste."[34]

Yet these "commercial filters" were the means of bridging the intellectual gap and bringing the formal elements of modern art down to a popular level. "Many people who are critical of modern art," the "Modern Art in Your Life" exhibition catalogue continued, "accept its parallels and offshoots in the field of design with familiar, even friendly, unconcern."[35] Such was the reaction of America's best-loved painter, Grandma Moses, when in an interview in 1950 she dismissed abstract art by allowing that "that sort of thing would be good for a rug or piece of linoleum."[36] While the creative energy of modern art was making for good press — most controversially, an article about Jackson Pollock in *Life* in 1949, which echoed a recent critical assessment by asking "Is he the greatest living painter in the United States?" — the magazine's readers did not see this kind of endeavor as "art." At best, *Life* admitted, they might have considered the tense drip patterns of Pollock's "action paintings" as "interesting, if inexplicable, decorations."[37] And, in fact, although most people would not accept the formalism, intellectualism, and expressionism that created the language of abstraction as the content of true art, they had no problem bringing its modern abstract vocabulary of amorphous shapes, drips and dabs, nervous linearity, and loose application of color into their homes. In that regard Grandma Moses did not go far enough. She should have added that along with rugs and linoleum, abstraction was also good for tabletops, curtains, and china, lampshades, upholstery, and virtually any other article of design that could be newly formed with a modern shape or be given a modern upbeat pattern. At a time when the modes of modernism had removed most contemporary art from the arena of popular accessibility, and when artists, particularly the young abstractionists in the United States, despaired over their isolation from public understanding,[38] design stepped in as a mediating element, returning a form of modernity based on artistic endeavors (however it may have trivialized them) to the public.

1   Advertisement for Masonite, *Interiors*, vol. 112 (August 1952), p. 38.
2   See George Nelson, "Modern Furniture ... An Attempt to Explore Its Nature, Its Sources, and Its Probable Future," *Interiors*, vol. 108 (July 1949), esp. pp. 108–11.
3   See Janet Kardon, ed., *Craft in the Machine Age, 1920–1945: The History of Twentieth-Century American Craft* (New York: Harry N. Abrams, in association with the American Craft Museum, 1995).
4   Wilhelm Wagenfeld, quoted in Magdalena Droste, *Bauhaus, 1919–1933* (Cologne: Benedikt Taschen, 1993), p. 80.
5   Gio Ponti, "Senza aggettivi," *Domus*, no. 268 (March 1952), p. 1; translated in Centrokappa, Milan, *Il design italiano degli anni '50* (Milan: IGIS Edizioni, 1981), p. 296.
6   See Kathryn B. Hiesinger and George H. Marcus, *Landmarks of Twentieth-Century Design: An Illustrated Handbook* (New York: Abbeville Press, 1993), p. 143.
7   Hugh Casson, "Art by Accident: The Aesthetics of Camouflage," *Architectural Review*, vol. 96 (September 1944), p. 66.
8   Thomas Sheraton, *The Cabinet-Maker and Upholsterer's Drawing-Book*, 3rd ed. rev. (London, 1802), p. 378.
9   The undulant shapes of the tables used in the metal workshop at the Bauhaus in the 1920s, which in turn relate to nineteenth-century metalworkers' tables, were also noted as antecedent forms in Martin

Eidelberg, ed., *Design 1935–1965: What Modern Was* (Montreal: Musée des Arts Décoratifs, 1991), pp. 89, 346–47, note 118.

10 *This Week*, May 25, 1947, quoted by Eva Zeisel, Letter to the Editor, *Interiors*, vol. 109 (March 1950), p. 8.

11 *Interiors*, vol. 109 (January 1950), p. 22.

12 "Shmoo" was also the nickname given to an organic-shaped wall telephone with a dial in its handset designed by Henry Dreyfuss and testmarketed by AT&T in 1958.

13 George Nelson, "Modern Furniture," cited above, pp. 102–4.

14 Museum of Modern Art, New York, *Good Design: An Exhibition of Home Furnishings Selected by the Museum of Modern Art, New York, for the Merchandise Mart, Chicago* (1953), inside cover.

15 George Nelson, "The Contemporary Domestic Interior," *Interiors*, vol. 109 (July 1950), p. 62.

16 Chris Ritter, "An Interior View: Paul McCobb," *Art Digest*, September 15, 1952, p. 19.

17 Eero Saarinen, in Aline B. Saarinen, ed., *Eero Saarinen on His Work: A Selection of Buildings Dating from 1947 to 1964*, rev. ed. (New Haven: Yale University Press, 1968), p. 66.

18 Quoted in *Ericsson Review*, vol. 33 (1956), p. 124.

19 "Milan Close-Up," *Industrial Design*, vol. 1 (December 1954), p. 106.

20 Max Bill, "The Bauhaus Idea: From Weimar to Ulm," in *Architects' Yearbook 5* (London: Elek Books, 1953), p. 32.

21 John and Marilyn Neuhart, Introduction, *Eames Design: The Work of the Office of Charles and Ray Eames* (New York: Harry N. Abrams, 1989), p. 8.

22 See *Casabella Continuità*, no. 203 (November–December 1954).

23 "1° Compasso d'Oro, 1954, 'Relazione della Giuria,'" in Palazzo delle Stelline, Milan, *Design & design* (May 29–July 31, 1979), p. 22.

24 "Sculptor-Designed Table," *Art News*, vol. 46 (May 1947), p. 36.

25 Harry Bertoia, quoted in Eric Larrabee and Massimo Vignelli, *Knoll Design* (New York: Harry N. Abrams, 1981), p. 71.

26 Centro Studio Triennale, Milan, *Ceramica alla 9ª Triennale di Milano* (Milan: Editoriale Domus, 1953), p. 6.

27 "Picasso-esque Pottery," *House and Garden*, vol. 102 (July 1952), p. 26.

28 John Goldsmith Phillips, "Art in Silk," *Art News Annual* (November 1950), part 2, p. 172.

29 Many of these are documented by Dilys Blum, curator of costume and textiles at the Philadelphia Museum of Art, in an unpublished manuscript, "Painting by the Yard: American Artist-Designed Textiles 1947–57."

30 See "Great Art and Fashion Fabrics: The Saga of Dan Fuller and Five Modern Masters," *American Fabrics*, no. 35 (Winter 1955–56), pp. 51–55.

31 See Gio Ponti, "Astrattismo per una facciata," *Domus*, no. 267 (February 1952), pp. 2–3, 61; Eleanor Bittermann, *Art in Modern Architecture* (New York: Reinhold Publishing, 1952); and Paul Damaz, *Art in European Architecture* (New York: Reinhold Publishing, 1956).

32 Robert Goldwater in collaboration with René d'Harnoncourt, *Modern Art in Your Life*, Museum of Modern Art Bulletin (special issue), vol. 17 (1949), p. 5.

33 Max Bill, *Form: A Balance Sheet of Mid-Twentieth-Century Trends in Design* (Basel: Karl Werner, 1952), p. 11.

34 James Thrall Soby, "Mural-Scrolls," *Arts & Architecture*, vol. 66 (April 1949), p. 26.

35 Goldwater and d'Harnoncourt, *Modern Art*, cited above, p. 5.

36 Quoted in Saul Pett, "Grandma Moses, 90 This Week and Feeling Fine, Sniffs at Art Fame and Keeps Right on Painting," *Tulsa Sunday World Magazine*, September 3, 1950, p. 9.

37 "Jackson Pollock: Is He the Greatest Living Painter in the United States?," *Life*, August 8, 1949, p. 42.

38 See Mark Rosenthal, *Abstraction in the Twentieth Century: Total Risk, Freedom, Discipline* (New York: Guggenheim Museum, 1996), p. 122.

79 "Homemaker" plate designed by Enid Seeney (British), 1956-57. Glazed pottery. Made by Ridgway Potteries. Author's collection.

Modern — or Contemporary?

"To be contemporary," *House Beautiful* instructed its readers as the year 1955 began, "is to relax in the 20th Century, to avoid completely the modern strain of straining to be modern."[1] The magazine was fed up with the tiresome concerns that came with being modern, that is, with the strain of binding America's lifestyle to the austere aesthetic of an earlier generation at a time when the expanding economy, burgeoning industry, and dazzle of advertising offered so many temptations in the realm of material goods and design possibilities. In his book on interior decoration written the same year, the American designer William Pahlmann also noted a move away from the enduring values that defined good design toward another approach to modern that he too called "contemporary," which for him was transitory, less circumscribed in its definition, and comprised "styles from diverse periods and places." "Contemporary," he wrote, "means being *in keeping with the time you live in*. … Modern can be quickly dated. But contemporary implies change, improvement, addition and elimination — a steady editing of the existing set up, a changing of surroundings as you and your times change. This doesn't mean that you have to throw away all your furniture and start over every few years, but it does mean that you give to your surroundings the furbishing you reasonably give to your wardrobe or your automobile."[2] These attempts to distinguish what was modern from what was contemporary clearly reflected a conflict in design at mid-decade. Although there was no agreement on the usage of these two terms (historically, the preference was reversed in Great Britain), the balance between the definition of "modern" as good design on the one hand, and as a more permissive and ecumenical style on the other, came to be weighted more and more toward the latter in the years that followed.

A New Romanticism

Whatever limited popularity good design had achieved during the postwar years evaporated by mid-decade, and any expectations that it would gain further converts among the broad middle-level audience failed to materialize in the face of competition from the products of prosperity, whose dependence on a philosophy of consumption and upward mobility underscored Pahlmann's contemporary values of "change, improvement, addition and elimination." Home magazines no longer emphasized the kinds of simple, sturdy, and economical objects associated with good design, nor did furniture advertisements favor the term "modern" as an inducement to customers; "gracious" or "luxurious" was more likely to be chosen to describe the commodious living now being promoted. Less emphasis was placed on the modern style for houses in suburban developments, where there was a decided shift to the architectural trappings of colonial America (when Levitt's New Jersey community was built in 1958 the houses had colonial-style facades[3]) and to furnishings that followed suit. Grand Rapids designers who had worked in the modern style were also pulling back, and many manufacturers of traditional furniture were dropping their modern lines. T. H. Robsjohn-Gibbings, always a bellwether of postwar commercial design, once again changed his mind. Complaining that it is the "bond with the past that is missing in so much of our new housing today, for we have been led to believe that anything from the eggcups to the landscape gardening must be 'modern'"[4] (an approach he himself had strongly

advocated a decade before), Robsjohn-Gibbings again led the industry, this time seeking out sources for design in other places and eras. As early as 1953 he had reintroduced classical motifs into his work, and by 1955, drawing on his memories and emotions, he chose the delicate arches and slender columns of the "courtyards of Pompeii and Spain, the missions of California"[5] as the theme of a brilliant new furniture line he created for Widdicomb (fig. 80). *House Beautiful* saw this as the herald of "a new era of Romanticism" and devoted nine pages to Robsjohn-Gibbings's new work as the vanguard of this movement, which it said was "reforging the broken link between the past and the present, and thus insuring a continuity with the future." It is difficult to comprehend today how the arcaded forms of the elegant dining table and the accompanying benches, sideboards, and breakfronts could have been considered so innovative that *House Beautiful* deemed this line of furniture a pivotal moment in the decade's design. But with its appearance and the rapprochement with tradition that it foretold, the

80   Dining table designed by T.H. Robsjohn-Gibbings, 1955. Wood. Private collection, Philadelphia.

magazine could gleefully sound the death knell of the modern style, the culmination of its decade-long campaign against the modernists' "almost neurotic dread of anything ornamented or decorative."[6] In 1953, the magazine's editor, Elizabeth Gordon, had stooped to McCarthyite tactics to warn her readers about what she considered anti-American influences in modernism. "There is a well-established movement, in modern architecture, decorating, and furnishings," she wrote,

> which is promoting the mystical idea that "less is more." ... They are promoting unlivability, stripped-down emptiness, lack of storage space and therefore lack of possessions. ... This well-developed movement has social implications, because it affects the heart of our society — the home. Beyond the nonsense of trying to make us want to give up our technical aids and conveniences for what is *supposed* to be a better and more serene life, there is a social threat of regimentation and total control. ... *House Beautiful* finally speaks up to point plainly to the nonsense that goes on in the name of "good design." ... We still operate on common sense and reason. We know that less is *not* more. It is simply less![7]

Now, with the return of elements of tradition and ornament in the Robsjohn-Gibbings line, the magazine could inform its readers that the modern aesthetic had "played itself out. As elimination followed elimination, design was reduced to less and less. 'Modern' as it has been known in the last few decades, soon became incapable of anything but repetition of a few geometric forms. Designers have failed to find any inspiration in it as a point of view or departure."[8]

A new romanticism also emerged in the structures of Edward Durell Stone, an architect

81 Chair designed by Roberto Gabetti (Italian) and Aimaro d'Isola (Italian), 1956. Beech and upholstery. Made by Colli.

who had earlier contributed significantly to the modernist movement in America, collaborating on the glass and marble International Style Museum of Modern Art building in New York in 1937, the most advanced design in the city at the time. In 1954, taking his cue from Indian architectural traditions, he sheathed his United States embassy in New Delhi with ornamental pierced screens, and used decorative grillwork to give a glittering image to the round United States pavilion at the Brussels World's Fair in 1958. These were buildings that received considerable praise, unlike his venture into a more descriptive historicism, the Venetian-style Gallery of Modern Art on New York's Columbus Circle designed in 1958. In Italy a number of prestigious architects and designers were also looking to the past for inspiration, particularly to the turn-of-the-century Art Nouveau style (which was then being re-evaluated internationally through exhibitions and publications), and its organic style was made to seem particularly relevant to the forms of art and design in the 1950s.[9] Referred to as Neoliberty (from "Liberty," the Italian name for Art Nouveau), these buildings and furnishings (fig. 81) were seen from abroad as a retreat from and a betrayal of the postwar impulse for social responsibility and the modernist aesthetic of formal purity. The British critic and editor of the *Architectural Review*, Reyner Banham, could find no valid justification for this revival and claimed that it called "the whole status of the Modern Movement in Italy in question,"[10] but by this point modern was simply expanding, making way for the infusion of new inspiration, some of which was now coming from the past.

The melding of past and present, antique and modern, was nowhere more confidently carried out than in the opulently theatrical hotels designed by Morris Lapidus. In his modern Fontainebleau in Miami Beach, he liberally combined ancient statuary and antiques with pierced, free-form shapes and up-to-date materials to create interiors flush with the expression of glamour in a style that he called "modern French Provincial" (fig. 82)[11] but which critics lambasted as indulgent kitsch, appealing to popular, *nouveau riche* taste and a travesty of what architecture should be. While Lapidus wanted his brash hotels to be "no place like home," one element would have been familiar to many of the guests, the blending of the old and the new. Regardless of whether modern or period graced their homes up north, the furnishings would most likely have been found in newly built or newly redone interiors constructed and decorated with the products of the modern building and decorating industries — plate glass windows, masonite and plywood paneling, linoleum floor coverings, foam-rubber upholstery, synthetic furnishing fabrics, flat

82   Lobby of the Fontainebleau Hotel, Miami Beach, Florida, designed by Morris Lapidus (American), 1955. Courtesy Karlsberger/ Lapidus.

moldings, and new types of paint in the latest colors. Encouraged by decorating advice such as Pahlmann's and by national programs such as Operation Home Improvement (which was in full swing in 1956), homeowners were caught up in the spirit of redecorating, renovating their houses and replacing their heavy, prewar period reproductions with light, new, traditional or modern furniture, much of it from Grand Rapids. Regardless of the style of their furnishings, the contemporaneity of these interiors was unmistakable, as Alfred Auerbach, professor of marketing at the Pratt Institute in Brooklyn, had sarcastically pointed out in a speech in 1950: "Cape Cod houses and Georgian manor houses and low rambling ranch houses are all punctuated with picture windows — and presto, they are modern!"[12]

A 1955 Armstrong advertisement depicting "the modern fashion in floors" (fig. 83) shows a generic split-level interior with little architectural detailing, light walls, and beige tile floors that by then might have been found in any suburban house independent of its exterior style. It is furnished with woven area rugs and matting, Scandinavian and other modern-style furniture, nubby upholstery, woven draperies across the picture windows, unornamented china and metalware, a metal tripod lamp with nine lights, a large potted plant, and a stylized modern landscape painting in matching colors. The summation of tasteful, middle-class modern, partaking of many elements of good design, this interior could as easily have been furnished in the French Provincial or Early American period styles or with Robsjohn-Gibbings, Paul McCobb, or even Saarinen modern designs. This is what the Willet furniture company bragged about when it presented a "blending of past and present" in its new "Transitional"

the modern fashion in floors

You can remember—it wasn't long ago—when a beautiful room could have a floor that was luxurious—or practical. Never both. But now, new modern plastic floors like Armstrong Custom Corlon Tile combine the two wonderfully. Here's the luxury of soft delicate colorings, a wide range of tones that sparkle with the clear beauty of vinyl plastic. Here is the luxury of quietness and cushioned comfort underfoot. And here also is great practicality, for Custom Corlon Tile is one of the very few floors you can install anywhere, from basement to attic. You can use it, for example, on all levels of a split-level house, to give an effect of spaciousness by carrying a single floor throughout. Here is easy care at its easiest, too. A smooth surface that's quickly swept and resists spilled things. Wherever you use it, all through the house, Armstrong Custom Corlon Tile is the modern fashion in plastic floors.

Free portfolio describes this living-dining area in a modern split-level home. Sketch plan and list of furnishings included. Just send a post card to Armstrong Cork Company, 5511 Plum Street, Lancaster, Pennsylvania.

FLOORS

line that year. "What's really wonderful about Transitional," the advertisement read, "is its matchless ability to fit in with existing decorative schemes, or to establish exciting new ones. With a mere switch in accessories, Transitional can transform rooms from cozy colonial to spacious modern."[13]

The Romantic attitude that emerged from a renewed appreciation of the past resulted in an "increasingly hazy division between modern and traditional," a review of the "Today in Tradition" exhibition at the Merchandise Mart in Chicago in 1954 said. But it was a tradition, the reviewer added, that was flourishing, "not by virtue of a static obeisance to the past, but rather because of the acute awareness of the needs of today, reflected in the deliberate

83   "The Modern Fashion in Floors," advertisement for Armstrong floors, *American Home,* November 1955.

124

decorative and functional modifications being made in traditional forms and motifs." The introduction of modern had influenced all commercial furniture, even traditional pieces, which the reviewer noticed had come to "reflect an awareness of the requirements of contemporary life with lighter finishes, smaller scales, functional and decorative modifications retaining the effect of the past with [a] modern frame of reference."[14]

Another Modern

One thing that abetted the rage to refurbish was the reappearance of color, which for *Industrial Design* in 1955 was the "most conspicuous symbol of a new turn in designing and consuming. The new use of color, sometimes bizarre, often crosses our notions of suitability," the magazine admitted in its review of the highlights of the year, "but as we discover that our notions have changed, the new color seems more appropriate."[15] Pink, red, orange, and blue predominate in another Armstrong interior (color plate 17), which shows a finished basement decorated with striated multicolored tile flooring, a striped staircase, a textured simulated-stone fireplace, and furnished with a soda fountain, bar stools, foam seating, and a wooden platform table by George Nelson (see fig. 24) painted deep blue, like no good design object ever would have been. Conceived by Armstrong to show imaginative possibilities for its floor tiles, this original, playful, and colorful interior disregarded all the precepts that Edgar Kaufmann had outlined and suggested a new path for modern decorating free from any reference to period styles and free from the rules of good design as well. But this approach did not reject good design, it improved on it. Interiors of this type often embraced its

84 "Marshmallow" sofa designed by George Nelson, 1956. Painted metal with vinyl and foam rubber upholstery. Made by Herman Miller. Baltimore Museum of Art. Gift of Terri and Erwin Harris, Baltimore, by exchange.

85 "Tulip" chair designed by Eero Saarinen, 1956. Fiberglass, aluminum, and upholstery. Made by Knoll. Philadelphia Museum of Art. Gift of Gregory M. Harvey.

commonplace devices — wiry metal legs for table and chair supports, molded plywood and plastic for seating, foam-cushions, free-forms for tables and counters, wall storage components, organic-shaped decorative accessories — borrowing, reworking, reinterpreting, and coloring them to create a heightened form of modern. This popular style of decorating was not destined for the still often formal areas of the middle-class suburban house — living room, dining room, and master bedroom — where the stolid modern or traditional styles of Widdicomb, Baker, and Dunbar were secure, but was promoted for kitchens and dinettes, patios, TV rooms, family rooms, and finished basements — areas where the period's informal entertaining, its television watching, cocktail parties, barbecues, and card games took place.

As seen in the advertisement, the work of well-known designers, such as George Nelson, could sometimes be very comfortably enlisted for these spaces. Nelson, influential as a spokesperson for the rationality of good design, had frequently found his own creations

86 Handkerchief bowl designed by Paolo Venini (Italian), 1951. Blown glass. Made by Venini. Philadelphia Museum of Art. Gift of Venini S.p.A.

87 Handkerchief bowl made by Chance Manufacturing, English, 1950–55. Author's collection.

on the fringe of good design acceptance. The quirky forms of his curved-wedge-shape "Cocoanut" chair and his "Marshmallow" sofa put together from bar-stool cushions (fig. 84) challenged the limits of that aesthetic (although not the good design precept of engineering for the capabilities of industry), and seemed to fit more readily into this heightened milieu. Eero Saarinen's sculptural, molded-plastic pedestal chair (fig. 85) and its accompanying table, the last significant series of organic furniture to be fully embraced by good design, was also ripe for insertion into this environment, directly or in the form of imitations, as its flowing tulip shape was widely adapted and reinvented for dinette sets and leisure seating.

Had popular designers not revered what modern art and design had achieved, they would not have relied on it so heavily as inspiration for their own creations. The borrowing, exaggerating, and extending of modern forms occurred all over, with the worldwide application of bent-plywood techniques following the designs of Charles Eames as an early and significant example. Glass factories in many countries became infatuated with the lively, colorful and expressive asymmetrical shapes that were blown at the furnaces of Murano. Fulvio Bianconi's and Paolo Venini's freely shaped "Handkerchief" bowls (fig. 86) were, for example, mimicked (albeit in a regularized form) in thick glass bowls with transfer-decoration manufactured by Chance in England (fig. 87). The work of well-known painters and sculptors was also imitated. Alexander Calder's mobiles, with their steel arms and abstract sheet-metal shapes painted in primary colors, were endlessly appropriated for design; they inspired everything from the

configurations of Italian lamps with colorful
glass globes to decorative metalwork and
patterns on textiles of all types. A
monochromatic image of a mobile appears
almost as a large-scale photographic
reproduction on an anonymous American
textile (fig. 88), while another American fabric
interprets Calder more imaginatively,
intermingling mobile-like arching black lines
and flat, colored areas with calligraphic
swashes and triangular and global shapes
(color plate 13). The lively designs of Joan Miró
were also a frequent source, interpreted in one
instance as a small-scale repeat on a printed
cotton from Germany (color plate 14). But more
often the inspiration was indirect, subtly
alluding to the wealth of artistic innovations that
were unveiled during the era. The strong linear
statements of many 1950s abstractions, from the
dense gestural drip patterns in Jackson Pollock's
monumental paintings to the more lyrical

88   Printed fabric, American, 1950s.
Philadelphia Museum of Art. Purchased with
funds contributed by an anonymous donor.

89 Sugar bowl and creamer, American, 1950s. Glass. Made by Hazel-Atlas. Author's collection.

calligraphic expressions created by such foreign artists as Georges Mathieu in Paris, reemerged at a distance — as lines of fluid color encased in Italian and Norwegian glass, or as repetitive "doodles" printed on American popular lampshades or woven in fabrics, like the one that covers a biomorphic three-legged chair from Sweden (color plate 15). These decorative intertwinings were immensely popular and spilled over to ornament a wealth of other objects, not all restricted to modern styles (fig. 89). The familiar voids of Henry Moore reasserted themselves in decorative ceramics, such as the large series of inventive forms made by Lusso (color plate 16), and the wiry spatial descriptions and stringing of constructivist sculpture were suggested in bases and supports of ashtrays, bowls, planters, and lamps, and in the decorative patterns of parallel lines that were frequently used on pottery, glass (figs. 50, 87), and textiles.

Emblematic of the popular esteem given to modern design was the way it was depicted by others, appealing to those who had a desire for modernity but did not want to purchase such objects for their homes. This sentiment was clearly expressed in an American advertisement for the "Fantasy" tableware pattern made by Red Wing, an easy-to-take pastel design showing floral motifs over free-form solids, which was billed as the "answer to those who 'love modern but simply can't live with it'."[16] Enid Seeney's lively "Homemaker" dinnerware (fig. 79),[17] designed 1956-57, brought a whiff of modernity to newly style-conscious British homemakers, who could feel right up-to-date setting their tables with images of the latest in furniture design, boomerang shapes, wiry accessories, and spindly lines without having to commit fully to contemporary

129

furnishings. The "Homemaker" service, which was created to emulate the success of modern tableware in the United States, was produced exclusively for Woolworth's in Britain beginning in 1957. The design depicts two pieces of furniture that can actually be identified, an armchair by Robin Day and a double settee by the Swedish designer Sigvard Bernadotte, along with a sideboard that closely parallels one designed by Gordon Russell, but the other pieces convincingly translate the vocabulary of international modern design into a similarly British mold. The trappings of modernity could also be called up for consumers in other comfortable and inexpensive ways, as the Swedish designer Stig Lindberg did when he whimsically offered his own decorative pottery lined up on shelves on a furnishing fabric (fig. 90), while modern lighting — spots, plastic bubbles, perforated metal wall fixtures, hanging lamps — could be enjoyed as images drawn with nervous linearity on an English wallpaper from Sanderson (fig. 91). One did not actually have to buy the requisite planter

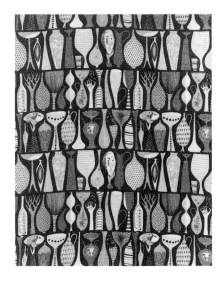

90 "Pottery," printed fabric designed by Stig Lindberg (Swedish), c. 1947. Made by Nordiska Kompaniet. Montreal Museum of Decorative Arts. Gift of Geoffrey N. Bradfield.

91 "Illuminata," printed wallpaper designed by M. Cinderby (British), 1956. Made by Sanderson. The Whitworth Art Gallery, The University of Manchester (reproduced with permission of Arthur Sanderson & Sons Ltd).

92　"Bowls and Planters of Lifetime Fiberglas,"
advertisement for Kimball Manufacturing
(detail), *Interiors*, August 1955.

93　"Park Avenue" (*Philodendron monstera*),
machine-printed wallpaper, Canadian, 1953.
Cooper-Hewitt, National Design Museum,
Smithsonian Institution/Art Resource, New York.
Gift of Suzanne Lipschutz.

advertised by Fiberglas as a "practical answer
to contemporary decorative needs!" (fig. 92);
a carefree philodendron could be had in a
large, bold form on a Canadian wallpaper
(fig. 93), or, alternatively, on the "Homemaker"
service, or on another British tableware pattern,
"Plant Life," designed by Terence Conran for
Midwinter around 1956 and depicting actual
pieces sold in his stores. [18]

Another important source of modern imagery
for design was to be found in science and
technology, from crystallography (the Festival
Pattern; see fig. 59) to rocketry (which was
particularly fertile for automotive styling and
advertising). A naïve wonderment at the
marvels of television brought a literal depiction
of this new technology to a pattern for
wallpaper (fig. 94). It not only shows the towers
that transmitted and relayed the signals and the
antennas that received them (along with the
sports and cultural events imagined as the heart
of television programming) but also portrays the
signals themselves, the modern rhythmical lines
that spread through the atmosphere and
broadcast these events to homes in the city and
across the countryside. A universal abstract

131

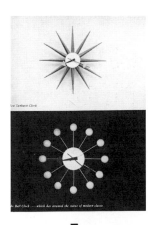

94 "Television," screen-printed wallpaper designed by Mildred C. McNutt (American), 1951. Made by Wall Trends. Cooper-Hewitt, National Design Museum, Smithsonian Institution/Art Resource, New York. Gift of Mildred C. McNutt.

95 Wall clocks designed by George Nelson, advertisement for Howard Miller, *Interiors*, October 1954.

motif originated in science in the form of atomic energy, which spoke to both the fears and the hopes of the modern era. The atom was chosen as a theme for several international exhibitions during the period, and gave rise at the time of the Festival of Britain in 1951, for example, to a large decorative screen composed of cells and balls on rods representing the carbon atom, which was created in front of London's science museum, and to the Atomium, an atomic model of gargantuan proportions that was the symbol and focal point of the Brussels World's Fair in 1958. The "Ball" — or "Atom" — wall clock with twelve balls on spokes, designed by George Nelson in 1949 (fig. 95; shown in an advertisement with other droll designs in his series of appliqué clocks for Howard Miller),

became a classic evocation of the decade's decorative preoccupation with the atom. Similar balls were also frequently found as lighthearted but useful additions to other objects, such as feet on appliances (figs. 44, 102) and chairs (fig. 68), and as ornamental accessories, like those on the metal arms that erupt from the stacked and layered biomorphic shapes on a French wall lamp (fig. 96). They also became multicolored clichés as coat hooks, used by Charles Eames for his children's "Hangitall" (1953) and by many others, objects that found wide popularity in England and France (fig. 97). Even Scalamandre, the conservative American textile firm best known for its traditional patterns and reproduction designs for historic houses, took up this theme; in 1952 it featured an atomic print that the *Atlanta Journal* pronounced as "new and up-to-date as the next blast in New Mexico" and described as "bursting with energy — atomic energy. Atoms, neutrons, protons, (or whatever they are) and chain reactions dance all over the fabric in a fanciful geometric design."[19]

Consumer Modern

William Pahlmann's definition of "contemporary" as the "steady editing of the existing set

96   Wall lamp, advertisement for M. Kobis/
R. Lorence, *Art & Decoration*, no. 55, 1956.

97   Coat hook, French, 1950s. Painted
wood and metal. Author's collection.

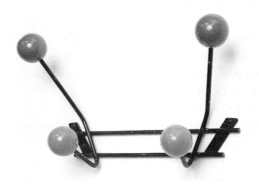

up," the "changing of surroundings as you and your times change," was another trend noted by *Industrial Design* in 1955: "In areas formerly marked by cautious investment for lifetime compatibility," the magazine explained, "a new attitude seems to have overtaken the consumer: he or she is less inclined to select a vacuum cleaner or water heater as if it were a mate for life. For the fact of the matter is, a purchase is seldom for keeps. If the kitchen is primrose pink (color plate 18) the housewife may grow tired of it, but in the back of her mind she knows that someday she'll get another one — so *why not?*"[20] This change in attitude, which the magazine quickly spotted and attributed to the onslaught of prosperity in America, seemed to apply equally to houses and household furnishings as to automobiles and appliances. Rejecting the considerations of economy and durability previously relied upon when household purchases had been contemplated and accepting America's expanding marketing ploy of planned obsolescence, consumers were now taking a devil-may-care approach that reflected the speed and mobility of contemporary life in which the average suburbanite changed residences every three or four years, confident that any mistakes could be rectified when the next buying opportunity came around.

By the mid-1950s, the future of an upwardly mobile suburbia was no longer in question. The extreme housing shortage and the economic instabilities that in 1949 had trapped Charles Mergendhal's young marrieds in a hastily built development no longer rang true; now, suburban communities, dotted with larger, more luxurious homes and bursting with bright new products, brought status to their residents — along with the continuing pressures of conformity and an awakening awareness of racial inequality and social injustice. John McPartland's *No Down Payment* (1957) depicts such a development, Sunrise Hills, in California. It had five thousand houses, "all of them new, with redwood, fieldstone and glass, all of them with patios and shining kitchens, television sets, automatic washers and dryers, automatic mixers, coffee-makers, toasters, garbage disposal gadgets, clock radios, freezer cabinets, automatic lawn sprinkling systems, electric lawnmowers, dishwashing machines," and residents who "never knew the price of anything big they bought — only the size of the monthly payments."[21]

The 1950s saw enormous changes in the marketing of these appliances; color was applied liberally, especially to heavy appliances (color plate 18), many of which were manufactured by corporations closely allied with the automobile industry. General Electric reported that 18 percent of the appliances sold in 1955 were in color, the favorite being "petal pink." Kitchen appliances had been available in colors earlier, but by mid-decade the variety of interior and exterior colors and their combinations, like those on automobiles, was far reaching. Automobiles themselves displayed the most conspicuous use of color, with Chrysler, for example, offering a "record choice of 58 exterior colors and 86 two-tone color combinations" in 1954.[22] The automobile, the decade's most singular and highly visible consumer product, headed discussions about American design throughout the Fifties, although the visual concerns, however controversial, were surpassed by others, such as power, reliability, obsolescence, and the manipulation of the consumer through the use of mass psychology in advertising.[23] But battles raged over the increasing size and elaboration of each year's automobiles; the bold excrescences of tail fins and bumpers and grandiose chrome ornamentation suggesting the gleaming, aerodynamic forms of air and space transport brought the greatest complaints, but color too offended with its wide range and flamboyance. At the same time a deliberate attempt was made to engage the female consumer with fine finishes, special colors, and elegant fabrics that sported abstract patterns and metallic filaments (fig. 98) to reflect "the atmosphere and comfort of the living room."[24] Advertisements insistently connected these luxurious fittings with designer fashions and expensive jewelry in aristocratic surroundings, as shown in one advertisement in which a model wearing an ensemble by Jacques Fath, a jeweled necklace from the Fifth Avenue merchant Harry Winston, and the enameled Cadillac crest are included to demonstrate that "Cadillac offers more of *everything* to make a woman happy" (fig. 99).[25]

Automobiles influenced other aspects of appliance design, notably the forms of their controls and the marks of their manufacturers, and their prominent placement. When several appliances were shown in 1955 at the "Good Design" exhibitions in an attempt to broaden their representation of everyday objects, marks were the subject of a disclaimer in the catalogue, which stated that "the maker's name or symbol was considered conspicuously out of key with the admired general design of each product."[26] For a copywriter for Plexiglas, however, it was the brilliance of colored plastic (which had replaced stamped enameled metal for many automobile insignias early in the decade) that added the final "distinctive touch for fine products" (fig. 100). Marks with crowns,

98 "Taj Mahal," upholstery fabric designed for the Lincoln Continental by Marianne Strengell (American), 1959. Cotton, rayon, and polyester-encased metal strip. Made by Chatham. Philadelphia Museum of Art. Gift of the designer.

99 Advertisement for Cadillac, *House Beautiful*, February 1955.

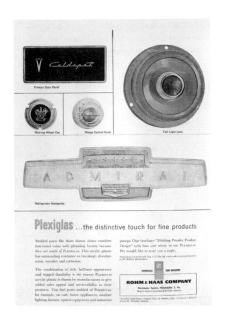

100 Plexiglas, advertisement for Rohm & Haas, *Industrial Design*, July 1955.

101 "Sony TR610" pocket radio, 1957. Plastic. Made by Tokyo Telecommunications Engineering Corporation. Philadelphia Museum of Art. Gift of COLLAB: The Contemporary Design Group for the Philadelphia Museum of Art.

crests, and stylized jewels capitalizing on associations with the half-century-old Cadillac insignia (see fig. 99) and those of other expensive cars appeared on air-conditioner panels, range control knobs, and refrigerator nameplates.

Elements of automotive styling, such as saturated colors, metallic decoration, and regal insignia, were also adopted for smaller appliances, including tiny plastic radios like Zenith's "Royal 500" pocket model, which was likewise positioned in advertising as a fashion statement tied in with expensive jewelry (color plate 19). The diminutive scale of appliances made possible by the use of transistors, invented at Bell Laboratories in 1947, brought heavy competition into these markets, with numerous models manufactured in the United States and abroad. The four-inch-high "Sony" pocket radio introduced in 1957 was based on American design features (fig. 101), but in 1959, for the world's first all-transistor television set, a plastic thirteen-inch model, the company was emboldened to offer a novel form evoking aspects of traditional Japanese design. Televisions were among the hottest marketing commodities of the decade. Like radios and phonographs before them, they had at first been sold primarily as consoles, their cabinetry, whether Chippendale, Chinese, French Provincial (fig. 2), Sheraton, or Modern, as much a consideration as performance and price. Rooms were furnished around television sets, which because of their size and weight and their connection to outdoor antennas had little flexibility and could not easily be moved. These restraints prompted the creation of models such as Philco's "Predicta" (fig. 102) with a separate picture tube on top of the chassis that could pivot and be seen from anywhere in a room (similar designs were produced in France, England, and Italy). But an alternative market for second models and greater flexibility was growing, and a new type emerged, one that was freed from cabinetry and made of metal or plastic, often with two-tone styling and considered portable no matter how unwieldy it may have been (as General Electric realized when it provided a large, obvious handle to emphasize the portability of its thirty-two-pound 1955 model; fig. 103). These sets were rivaled by even smaller, truly portable models, some in bright colors and with gold accents, such as the "Personal" television made by RCA Victor in 1956 (color plate 20).

Gold, gilt, and the shine of metallics were the finishing touches given to these appliances,

102　"Predicta" television, 1958. Plastic and brass housing with wooden cabinet. Made by Philco. Collection of Ron Kanter, Philadelphia.

103　Portable television, advertisement for General Electric, *American Home*, November 1955.

and they added a perceived value to a type of industrially conceived product designed for the home that likewise emerged from technological styling, such as the "Golden Triangle" carafe coffee server of 1957 made by Inland Glass (fig. 104). The creation of designer-engineers, it shows a fascination with hardware and a variety of materials that blend "functional beauty" with an implied "luxury," the fusing of 22-carat gold diamond-shape accents on heat-resistant glass. Gold was a commodity applied to other domestic objects, such as Shawnee's gold-splattered ceramic "Flight" ashtrays of pink, turquoise, and black, sold through five-and-ten-cents stores (fig. 105). These had a brilliant glossy sheen achieved with sprayed industrial applications, which were introduced along with lacquers instead of glazes in an effort to create products that were both American and contemporary, products that were distinctive and could compete with the cheaper ceramic and plastic objects flooding in from Japan.[27]

Many critics found the flashy design of American automobiles and popular home furnishings objectionable, cynical products of corporate design teams out to convince the public to replace products they already had with newer, better ones that sported additional features and an even more glittery appearance. The fascination that these American products seemed to have for those in other countries was particularly repugnant to some foreign critics, who decried the ennobling of the "tasteless" products of American mass culture, which they felt were taking their toll on international culture with the support of advertising and the media.

But Reyner Banham, and a few of his European colleagues, took another point of view; they not

104   "Golden Triangle" carafe, advertisement for Inland Glass, *American Home,* October 1957.

105   "Flight" ashtray, American, c. 1955–60. Ceramic. Made by Shawnee Pottery. Author's collection.

only glorified American consumer culture, its advertising and automobiles, but also took them as topics of serious consideration. In "A Throw-Away Esthetic," an article first published in 1955, Banham sought to justify the ephemeral brilliance and blatant symbolism of these products by explaining to his readers, who were more accustomed to discussions of design in terms of theoretical and formal functionalist aesthetics, that the "criticism of popular arts depends on an analysis of content, an appreciation of superficial rather than abstract qualities, and an outward orientation that sees the history of the product as an interaction between the sources of the symbols and the consumer's understanding of them." And, he continued, "the function of these symbol systems is always to link the product to something that is popularly recognized as good, desirable or exciting — they link the dreams that money can buy to the ultimate dreams of popular culture,"[28] much as Morris Lapidus had done in his hotels.

Writing in *Industrial Design* in 1959, another British observer, Ursula Townley Hansen, postulated what a future historian might make of all this:

> "Function, efficiency, and economy" are already strictly irrelevant (however desirable) to American design, because it is design for a rich world and a dream world. And so the historian of the shape of things may, in a sense, find more "honesty," more "significance," in those shapes which most offend us now. He will be more concerned to ask how much these shapes reflected the ideals and obsessions of a truly fantastic age, when the conquest of space in all its aspects seemed important, and mice and men whirled in orbit round the earth. But most important of all, he will be ready to detect in the "American" shapes of car rear-ends and juke boxes and non-sheer-line

refrigerators a quality that ranks in his eyes even above beauty, function, efficiency and economy: and enthusiasm for *invention*. He will admit that this was not always accompanied by an equal *capacity* for invention, but he will rejoice that the two came together often enough.[29]

The impact of American consumer culture was also felt by a considerable number of artists, who reacted to it in different ways. Throw-away consumerism, epitomized by the planned obsolescence of the automobile, was controverted by John Chamberlain in the United States and César in France, who rescued the detritus of car culture — the rusted junkyard remains of body and motor parts — and compacted it into powerful, colorful, monumental sculptures. Comic books, magazines, advertising, popular music, and consumer products fascinated members of the Independent Group in London, Richard Hamilton among them. He used such popular imagery as collage fragments and design sources for his own works, which expressed both admiration and irony in the appropriation of these elements. His consumer-crazed collage of 1956, *Just What Is It that Makes Today's Homes So Appealing?* (fig. 106), combines vignettes of popular Americana, from colorful appliances, a Ford insignia, and comic books to Al Jolson and a pin-up, in a classic agglomeration of consumer delights. In the United States, Pop art was also embracing product advertising and kitsch imagery, but with a seeming ambivalence about just what it was that made it so appealing to these artists. While many observers questioned the startling about-face that was altering the language of international contemporary art, which at that time was defined almost exclusively as abstraction, the influential American art critic

Harold Rosenberg recognized the social values
of kitsch and understood that exploiting the
figurative language and commercialism of
popular culture could be an energizing factor
for artists: "Using kitsch," he explained, "is one
of art's juiciest devices, and a comic revenge
for the looting of art by kitsch."[30]

106 *Just What Is It that Makes Today's
Homes So Appealing?* by Richard Hamilton
(British), 1956. Collage on paper. Kunsthalle,
Tübingen. Collection Professor Dr. Georg
Zundel.

1 "Resolution for 1955: Live the Contemporary Life!," *House Beautiful,* vol. 97 (January 1955), p. 37.

2 William Pahlmann, *The Pahlmann Book of Interior Design* (New York: Thomas Y. Crowell, 1955), pp. 25–28.

3 Herbert J. Gans, *The Levittowners: Ways of Life and Politics in a New Suburban Community* (New York: Pantheon Books, 1967), p. 270.

4 T. H. Robsjohn-Gibbings, *Homes of the Brave* (New York: Alfred A. Knopf, 1954), p. 110.

5 Joseph A. Barry, "A New Era of Romanticism Is Here," *House Beautiful,* vol. 98 (May 1956), p. 144.

6 Ibid., pp. 140–45, 196–98.

7 Elizabeth Gordon, "The Threat to the Next America," *House Beautiful,* vol. 95 (April 1953), pp. 126–27, 129.

8 Barry, "A New Era," cited above, p. 143.

9 See Ettore Sottsass, Jr., "Liberty: La bibbia di mezzo secolo," *Domus,* no. 292 (March 1954), pp. 43–45; and Edgar Kaufmann, Jr., "Art Nouveau and All That ... ," *Industrial Design,* vol. 5 (April 1958), pp. 38–40.

10 Reyner Banham, "Neoliberty: The Italian Retreat from Modern Architecture," *Architectural Review,* vol. 125 (April 1959), p. 232.

11 Morris Lapidus, *Too Much Is Never Enough* (New York: Rizzoli, 1996), p. 165.

12 Alfred Auerbach, speech to the Merchants & Manufacturers Club, Chicago, January 16, 1950, quoted in Terence Riley and Edward Eigen, "Between the Museum and the Marketplace: Selling Good Design," in *The Museum of Modern Art at Mid-Century: At Home and Abroad* (New York: The Museum of Modern Art, 1994), p. 169.

13 Advertisement, *House Beautiful,* vol. 97 (February 1955), p. 1.

14 L. W., "Today in Tradition," *Interiors,* vol. 113 (March 1954), pp. 90–91.

15 "Trends," *Industrial Design,* vol. 2 (December 1955), p. 35.

16 Quoted in Sheila Steinberg and Kate Dooner, *Fabulous Fifties: Designs for Modern Living* (Atglen, Pa.: Schiffer, 1993), p. 11.

17 See Simon Moss, *Homemaker: A 1950s Design Classic* (Moffat, Scotland: Cameron & Hollis, 1997).

18 See Alan Peat, *Midwinter: A Collectors' Guide* (Moffat, Scotland: Cameron & Hollis, 1992), pp. 44–45.

19 Alice Richards, "A-Power Energizes New Fabric," *Atlanta Journal,* June 9, 1952.

20 "Trends, 1955: The Meaning of New Traditions in Design," *Industrial Design,* vol. 2 (December 1955), p. 34. The new attitude toward consumption was thoroughly examined by Thomas Hine in *Populuxe* (New York: Alfred A. Knopf, 1986).

21 John McPartland, *No Down Payment* (New York: Simon and Schuster, 1957), pp. 82, 18.

22 Howard Ketcham, "Colors Car Buyers Want," *American Fabrics,* no. 28 (Spring 1954), p. 113.

23 See John Keats, *The Insolent Chariots* (Philadelphia: J. B. Lippincott, 1958).

24 Ketcham, "Colors Car Buyers Want," cited above, pp. 113–14.

25 See The Museum at the Fashion Institute of Technology, New York, "Driving Fashion: Automobile Fabrics of the 1950s" (June 24– October 4, 1977), brochure.

26 Museum of Modern Art, New York, *Good Design: An Exhibition of Home Furnishings Selected by the Museum of Modern Art, New York, for the Merchandise Mart, Chicago* (1955), n.p.

27 Jim Mangus and Bev Mangus, *Shawnee Pottery: An Identification & Value Guide* (Paducah, Kentucky: Collector Books, 1994), p. 11.

28 Reyner Banham, "A Throw–Away Esthetic," *Industrial Design,* vol. 7 (March 1960), p. 65.

29 Ursula Townley Hansen, "Taking America Straight," *Industrial Design,* vol. 6 (August 1959), p. 71.

30 Harold Rosenberg, "Pop Culture: Kitsch Criticism," in *The Tradition of the New* (New York: Horizon Press, 1959), p. 265.

107   "Kitchen Machine" designed by Gerd Alfred Müller (German), 1957. Polystyrol housing. Made by Braun. Collection Stefan Hauer.

Corporate Modern

By the end of the Fifties, modern seemed to be everywhere — on the street, in shops, at home, splashed across the pages of magazines, and flickering on the screens of the decade's great success, television. Even London's petty criminals warmed to it, at least as they were portrayed in the 1960 West End musical spoof *Fings Ain't Wot They Used T'be*. When the audience heard a decorator advise his cockney clients to do up their gambling den "Contemporary" — for "nowadays," he told them, "everything's modern"[1] — they could only have nodded in agreement, but conspiratorially, knowing as he undoubtedly did that the style of inventive, organic forms, abstract patterning, and craftlike furnishings was already out of fashion, among popular consumers as well as among the avant-garde. What persisted most universally of the modern experience was what was practical, the plain, rectangular, unarticulated shells that defined most new construction, the boxlike government offices, educational buildings, commercial high rises, and vanilla apartment houses that were transforming the cities and the suburbs — their pedestrian modern, stripped-down style by then as much of an economic windfall as an aesthetic preference. "Magazines, newspapers, museums, and all other sources of influence had so unanimously mounted the bandwagon," Jean Burchard and Albert Bush-Brown reported in their book *Architecture of America* in 1961, that "institutional buying of something that could at least be called contemporary design was so confirmed that the institution which bought conventionally bought modern."[2] And much of the modern they bought was conventional: glass, steel, and concrete buildings distinguished only by their uniformity and fitted out with uniform, generic, modern furnishings within.

George Nelson's tripartite aesthetic division of modern design into the machine, handicraft, and biomorphic looks no longer accurately distinguished progressive design, with the craftlike and the biomorphic being over-shadowed by a design that was on the one hand precise, technical, and corporate, and on the other, sleek and shiny — a revival of the machine imagery of decades before. The priorities of modern design had also changed, from economical products destined for the average home, a market that now seemed to be becoming saturated (or turning to sources in the past), to those meant for upscale and corporate clients. Charles Eames, for one, so committed to low-cost furnishings right after the war, took the technology for molding plywood in compound curves that he had applied to simple seating for the home (fig. 108) and utilized it for a complex product aimed at the high-end market, a swivel-based lounge chair and ottoman of shell construction made of expensive rosewood plywood and with leather for cushions (fig. 109). Prestigious designers

108 Chair designed by Charles Eames, 1945. Plywood and chromed steel. Made by Herman Miller. Philadelphia Museum of Art. Gift of Mrs. L. Talbot Adamson.

109 Lounge chair and ottoman designed by Charles Eames, 1956. Linated rosewood, aluminum, and leather upholstery. Philadelphia Museum of Art. Purchased with funds contributed by Mr. and Mrs. Adolph G. Rosengarten in memory of Calvin S. Hathaway.

were hired by a number of large corporations to create new products and identity systems, and to build new headquarters, such as Mies van der Rohe's Seagram Building in New York (1958), which would solidify their public image. Following the model of Olivetti in Italy, which for decades had been known for the quality of its design (including graphics by Giovanni Pintori and products by Marcello Nizzoli, joined toward the end of the 1950s by Mario Bellini and Ettore Sottsass, Jr.), the IBM corporation asked several celebrated designers — Charles Eames, Elliot Noyes, and Paul Rand among them — to redefine its image with identity systems, advertising, and product design, creating America's first integrated corporate design program. Noyes, whose first product for IBM had been a typewriter redesign in 1949, brought both organic design and smart colors into American office machinery with his "Selectric" typewriter in 1961 (fig. 110), following the inspiration of the expressive sculptural typewriters and sewing machines (fig. 56) created by Nizzoli (who had by then, however, turned to angular geometry for his own Olivetti products). Noyes's work was a crystallization of the expressive currents of the 1950s, filtered for corporate purposes, just when these forms had lost their force in advanced design circles.

A geometric functionalist design was preferred for corporate executive offices, with Knoll's Corporate Planning Unit under Florence Knoll the leading provider of tasteful anonymous design for these settings (fig. 111). The return of a second range of Mies van der Rohe's furniture to production in 1964, and the reintroduction of tubular-metal models from the 1920s by Le Corbusier, Charlotte Perriand, and Pierre Jeanneret, and by Marcel Breuer around

110   "Selectric" typewriter designed by Eliot Noyes (American), 1961. Made by I.B.M. Courtesy the IBM Corporation.

the same time, provided a wider choice of historic functionalist designs for these interiors and gave added impetus to the functionalist revival. These elegant pieces, conventional corporate status symbols and prestigious home furnishings, were reincarnated as the embodiment of "modern" design. The renewed interest in this style was abetted by a well-publicized design exhibition in 1958 at the Museum of Modern Art in New York, still unchallenged as the international arbiter of design, and by the opening of its first permanent design galleries in 1964, both of which emphasized the functionalist origin of the museum's design aesthetic. Leaving behind whatever ecumenicalism had been part of its "Good Design" exhibitions, the museum reverted to the glorification of the concept of machine-style design that could be traced back to prewar Germany. Writing in an introduction

111   Executive reception room in the CBS Building, New York, designed by Florence Knoll (American), 1962. Courtesy Knoll, Inc.

to the collection in 1959, Arthur Drexler, director of the department of architecture and design at the Museum of Modern Art, could once again define modern in these terms, repudiating the diversity, vitality, and validity of the entire past decade of design by asserting that "the shapes that most readily suggest the twentieth century are usually geometric, precisely finished, smooth, and without the elaboration and variety of detail we associate with the craftsman's handiwork."[3]

The functionalist revival — and its newly revalidated position as "modern" — continued to flourish in spite of the increasingly strident rejection of this approach by critics and designers, who attacked it from various points of view. Reyner Banham rejected the application of the functionalist aesthetic to product design on a conceptual level, decrying its "objective, absolute, universal and eternally valid" laws of form. "We live in a throw-away economy," he wrote, "a culture in which the most fundamental classification of our ideas and worldly possessions is in terms of their relative expendability. ... It is clearly absurd to demand that objects designed for a short useful life should exhibit qualities signifying eternal validity — such qualities as *divine* proportion, *pure* form or *harmony* of colors."[4] T. H. Robsjohn-Gibbings, for his part, rejected it on a level of style, seeing a return to the past as the only way to create a lively design for the future. "The taste of an old generation is dying, the taste of a new generation is being born," he wrote. "The taste that is dying can be defined in one word — 'modern.' ... For the new taste in interiors and furniture we must visualize the opposite of the modern white cube interior furnished with rigid formations of upholstered plastic and upholstered steel. ... In the heaped-up, period clutter there is something warm, secure and domestic in contrast to the cold inhuman modernity."[5]

Within the context of the modernist revival, designers sought distinct paths that would keep them from contributing to the fossilization of this style. One alternative was to broaden the functionalist vocabulary, as the Dane Arne Jacobsen did with his amalgamation of demonstrative organic forms with modernist materials in his furnishings (fig. 112) and interiors for the Scandinavian Airlines System Royal Hotel and Air Terminal in Copenhagen, completed between 1956 and 1960. Another approach evolved at the Hochschule für Gestaltung (Institute of Design) in Ulm, West Germany, where Max Bill continued, and even exaggerated, the Bauhaus aesthetic of pure, unornamented forms. Bill placed great emphasis on the design of everyday objects and the creation of prototypes for industry, and the school's collaborative production with the Braun manufacturing company originated the concept of product families that was demonstrated in Braun's line of cleanly styled radios, phonographs, and small appliances in wood and neutral tones of plastic (fig. 107). These cool, undecorated products, which followed the Bauhaus pursuit of essential forms but avoided the stylistic mannerisms of the functionalist past, became the outstanding icons of German design from the late 1950s, and their legacy of spare logical design is seen in many of the ordinary domestic products that we use today. In Italy, an approach equally reductive as Bill's, and equally divorced from broad popular taste, gave a breathtaking vitality to the products of the Milanese design firm Danese, founded in 1957. Drawing on a group of designers whose rationalist

112 "Swan" chair designed by Arne Jacobsen (Danish), 1957. Fiberglass, upholstered foam rubber, and chromed steel. Made by Fritz Hansen. Philadelphia Museum of Art. Purchased with the Marie Josephine Rozet Fund.

150

113 "Cubo" ashtray designed by Bruno Munari (Italian), 1957. Melamine and aluminum. Philadelphia Museum of Art. Gift of Jacqueline and Bruno Danese.

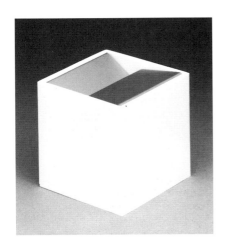

backgrounds and perfectionist bias melded with those of the firm, Danese created its own product aesthetic of sleek, perfect forms made with craft-based production techniques in metal and glass, and deftly in plastic (fig. 113). Similarly, the Italian plastics firm Kartell refined the forms of everyday objects, such as buckets and dish drains, into ideal types, for which it received many design accolades, although its products, like those of Braun and Danese, appealed mainly to an elite market.

The priority given to aesthetics, and to the designer as artist, shifted with the departure of Bill from the Ulm faculty in 1957, when a new philosophy brought mathematics, science, and ergonomics to challenge the reign of art in the modern design equation. With the increasing alienation of the artist from industrial design, according to the Ulm model and more and more in conventional corporate design offices, craftspeople were forced to rethink their position. They began to turn from the Bauhaus ideal of the craftsperson as designer of prototypes for factory production, which had given them employment in the postwar years, to concentrate on the goals of craftsmanship and personal expression. The 1950s and 1960s saw the emergence of a contemporary craft movement centered in the United States that applied traditional methods and aspects of the craft philosophy to the creation of one-of-a-kind, not production, objects, which eventually were to have little functional purpose and brought them into an uneasy alliance with art that has never been comfortably resolved.

The multivalent style that defined the Fifties — both the robust exploitation of technological advances such as the molding of plywood and plastic and the organic forms, pastel and fringe colors, and lively patterns that established its ornamental vitality — could not fail to serve as a magnet for those who later, especially toward the end of the 1970s, searched in the past for new sources of design. Postmodern designers at that time looked not only to classical and traditional styles but also to the more recent past. The Fifties found particular resonance among the designers of the Memphis group in Milan, organized in 1980, who exploited its decorative elements for textiles, plastic laminates, and graphics. But these and more recent nods to the period (as familiar as the aerodynamic flourishes of cigarette and sportswear logos and as knowing as the intricate, compound curves of a polyurethane and steel side chair by Philippe Starck, which makes formal reference to the plywood designs of Charles Eames and verbal reference to the entire decade with its name "Boom Rang"; fig. 114) in no way recaptured the spirit of the Fifties. For modernity was not just an adventure in style but, in the broadest expression of the period's aims, an attempt at using new forms, economical means, and up-to-date, accessible decoration in order to bring a better — and a modern — way of life to everyone.

1   The musical, *Fings Ain't Wot They Used T'be,* written by Frank Norman, with lyrics by Lionel Bart, opened at the Garrick Theatre in London on February 11, 1960. It had first been performed at the Theatre Royal in Stratford the previous year.
2   John Burchard and Albert Bush-Brown, *The Architecture of America: A Social and Cultural History* (Boston: Little, Brown, 1961), pp. 460–61.
3   Arthur Drexler, Introduction, in Arthur Drexler and Greta Daniel, *Introduction to Twentieth Century Design from the Collection of the Museum of Modern Art, New York* (Garden City, N.Y.: Doubleday, 1959), p. 6.
4   Reyner Banham, "A Throw-Away Esthetic," *Industrial Design,* vol. 7 (March 1960), pp. 62–63.
5   T. H. Robsjohn-Gibbings, "The New Taste," *Interior Design,* vol. 33 (November 1962), p. 172.

114   "Boom Rang" chair designed by Philippe Starck (French), 1992. Polyurethane and steel. Courtesy OLC, Philadelphia.

Les Années 50. Paris: Centre Georges Pompidou, 1988.

Eidelberg, Martin, ed. *Design 1935–1965: What Modern Was.* Montreal: Musée des Arts Décoratifs, 1991.

Gilbert, Anne. *40s and 50s Designs and Memorabilia: Identification and Price Guide.* New York: Avon Books, 1994.

Hiesinger, Kathryn B., and George H. Marcus, eds. *Design Since 1945.* Philadelphia: Philadelphia Museum of Art, 1983.

Hiesinger, Kathryn B., and George H. Marcus. *Landmarks of Twentieth-Century Design: An Illustrated Handbook.* New York: Abbeville Press, 1993.

Hillier, Bevis. *The Decorative Arts of the Forties and Fifties: Austerity/Binge.* New York: C. N. Potter, 1975.

Hine, Thomas. *Populuxe.* New York: Alfred A. Knopf, 1986.

Horn, Richard. *Fifties Style: Then and Now.* Philadelphia: Courage Books, 1988.

Jackson, Lesley. *The New Look: Design in the Fifties.* London: Thames and Hudson, 1991.

Jackson, Lesley. *"Contemporary": Architecture and Interiors of the 1950s.* London: Phaidon Books, 1994.

Lhamon, W. T., Jr. *Deliberate Speed: The Origins of a Cultural Style in the American 1950s.* Washington, D.C.: Smithsonian Institution Press, 1990.

Marcus, George H. *Functionalist Design: An Ongoing History,* Munich/New York: Prestel, 1995.

Marling, Karal Ann. *As Seen on TV: The Visual Culture of Everyday Life in the 1950s.* Cambridge, Mass.: Harvard University Press, 1994.

Marsh, Madeleine. *Miller's Collecting the 1950s.* London: Miller's, 1997.

Pulos, Arthur J. *The American Design Adventure, 1940–1975.* Cambridge, Mass.: Harvard University Press, 1988.

Steinberg, Sheila, and Kate Dooner. *Fabulous Fifties: Designs for Modern Living.* Atglen, Pa.: Schiffer, 1993.

Index of Names

Photographic Acknowledgments

Will Brown (Philadelphia): color plates 11, 12, 20; figs. 3, 34, 49, 51, 52, 54, 61, 63-65, 73, 79, 80, 87, 89, 97, 98, 102, 105, 109; Philippe De Gobert (Brussels): color plate 16; Richard P. Goodbody (New York): color plate 5; figs. 1, 42, 77, 90; Matthias Hauer (Munich): fig. 107; pp. 1, 159–160; Laurent-Sully Jaulmes (Paris): color plate 3; Ralph Lieberman (Williamstown, Mass.): fig. 74; Paul Marcus (Philadelphia): figs. 40, 78; Mark Meachem (New York): color plate 4; Willy Maywald (Paris): fig. 36; Eric Mitchell (Philadelphia Museum of Art): color plate 6; figs. 47, 75, 85, 88, 112; Sydney W. Newbery (London): fig. 29; Lynn Rosenthal (Philadelphia Museum of Art): color plates 8, 13; Anna Schamschula (Frankfurt): color plate 10; Atelier Schneider (Berlin): p. 158; Vitra Design Museum (Weil am Rhein): color plate 15; Ole Woldbye (Copenhagen): fig. 66; Graydon Wood (Philadelphia Museum of Art): figs. 45, 46, 48, 50, 58, 86, 101, 113

Following pages:
p. 158: "Little Man" fabric designed by Angelo Testa (American), 1942–43. Bauhaus-Archiv Berlin.

pp. 159–60: Plastic laminate, details of two trays, German, 1950s. Stadtmuseum Trostberg.

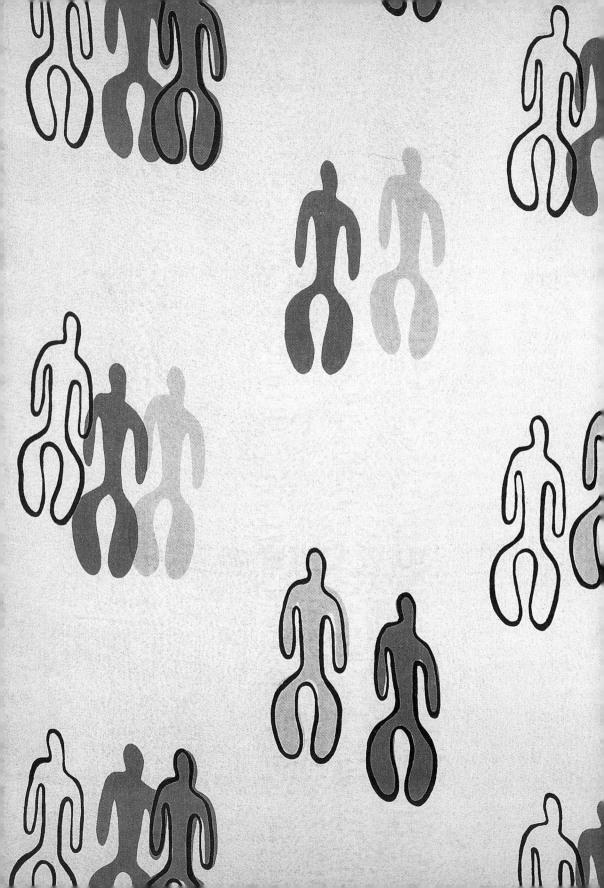